The Trust Factor

The Trust Factor

The Missing Key to Unlocking Business and Personal Success

Russell J. von Frank II

BEP
BUSINESS EXPERT PRESS
Leader in applied, concise business books

First published in 2020 by
Business Expert Press, LLC
222 East 46th Street, New York, NY 10017
www.businessexpertpress.com

ISBN-13: 978-1-95253-872-8 (paperback)
ISBN-13: 978-1-95253-873-5 (e-book)

Business Expert Press Business Career Development Collection

Collection ISSN: 2642-2123 (print)
Collection ISSN: 2642-2131 (electronic)

First edition: 2020

10 9 8 7 6 5 4 3 2 1

This book is dedicated to my wife Lisa whose encouragement and support over so many years inspired me to get this book finished. She is a true partner in every sense of the word, no man could want more. Most importantly she has shown me how trust can heal my wounded heart and make it grow far beyond that I could have ever imagined.

Abstract

The business world is changing rapidly externally and internally. Older forms of traditional corporate capitalism are being replaced with social capitalistic businesses. Traditional generations of employees are aging out of the workforce and being replaced by Gen X, Gen Y, Millennials, Gen Z, and now Gen Alpha. Each new generation is becoming less tolerant of the old school office environment. They want something new that provides a sense of connectedness, collaboration, and appreciation. That type of culture requires a solid foundation of trust to work effectively. Unfortunately, employee trust of leadership has sunk to an all-time low. Almost two-thirds of employees have little or no trust in management.

This book is designed to be a practical guide, resource, and workbook for CEOs, executives, managers, and employees to understand how trust is formed, where trust issues begin, why they are held on to, and how to work through them. Ultimately, the goal is to learn to effectively build a culture of trust within your business. Why, because all businesses have one thing in common—employees. They are people first, and workers second. They can no more separate from their personal issues and baggage when they come to work than you can separate your soul and your body. All their trust issues come with them and they don't check them at the door when they arrive at work. The lost productivity, impact on work environment, and general quality of life are immeasurable.

Trust is the very foundation upon which working and personal relationships are made and conducted. Without trust, nothing of importance happens. Trust is as personal as your fingerprints, so it is no wonder why building and sustaining trust in the workplace has been difficult to accomplish. Instead, it is easier to assume trust exists and everyone should act accordingly. This leads to miscommunications, unrealized expectations, lost efficiencies, hurt feelings, resentments, frustrations, and betrayals of assumed trust. All these negative feelings obstruct the ability of your workforce to work together and the cost to your bottom line is monumental. This book is designed to change all that.

Russ von Frank, MBA, EMT, is CEO, author, executive coach, trainer, speaker, and business consultant. Starting off as a Third Officer in the U.S. Merchant Marine and Ensign in the U.S. Navy Reserve, he went on to be a third-generation CEO of his family business. After 25 years he merged that business with another to spend more time on executive coaching and business consulting. Over 20 years he has logged in over 10,000 hours of coaching and consulting businesses of all sizes and industries. He holds two Bachelor of Science degrees, an MBA in Organizational Development, and several coaching certifications.

Keywords

betrayal; coaching; competence; confidence; conversation; core values; culture; emotional intelligence; empowerment; failure; forgiveness; growth; heartmath; integrity; leadership; positive intelligence; profitability; relationship; social capitalism; stakeholders; success; trust; trustworthy; vulnerability

Contents

Acknowledgments

I believe trust is what binds us together as people, as husbands, wives, children, parents, friends, and all those who touch our life in one way or another. This book has been 20 years in the making, through a lot of iterations as each person in turn has added value to the work.

This book would not have been possible if not for the encouragement, guidance, suggestions, honest feedback, and those who have listened to me talk about this concept over and over again.

To my daughter Samm who trusted me at a very young age to be her "second" dad without hesitation. There is nothing like the vulnerability of a child to help teach trust at the deepest levels.

Thank you to the TEC/Vistage coaches I have met along the way. I have learned so much from you and been inspired to be the best coach I can be. To Hal Cherney, Rick Martin, and Ole Carlson for putting my feet squarely on the coaching path. Ole, I just want you to know have learned to sing a different tune.

To the late Judith E. Glaser, her We Institute, Ben Croft, and the entire WBECS team for creating the Conversational Intelligence Certification program and most importantly to Judith for writing her book which brought so many great people together.

To my original Conversational Intelligence (C-IQ) cohort, Gail Basaraba, Wendy Eustace, and Ute Franzen-Waschke for your ideas and encouragement as I worked out my ideas. To my second C-IQ cohort, Trudy Ames, Ken Buch, Patricia Gifford, John Loche, Tammy Rowland, Elizabeth Ruppe, Christine Trani, and Stephane Wachman as I labored to pull my different thoughts together. I look forward to our next adventure together with Positive Intelligence© Thanks to all of you for listening over the past couple of years and encouraging me to keep writing. I value our time together and the opportunity to learn from all of you on a regular basis.

To my fellow C-IQ compatriots Ute Franzen-Waschke and Anita Edvinsson. Ute introduced me to Anita, and Anita introduced me to her publisher Rob Zwettler, Executive Acquisitions Editor at Business Expert Press. My thanks to Rob and his team who thought enough of my idea to agree to publish my book.

To Steve Ramerini and Compelceos for a place to work with CEOs on their businesses and Compel member Rakesh Bhargava who over a decade ago got me to agree in writing to write my book, I've never forgotten.

To John DeLalio and Keith Parker for their thoughts, comments, and suggestions to make this a better book. I am immensely grateful for your insight and experience.

To my clients and fellow coaches who have been willing to share their stories and bring depth to the examples I used to illustrate the points I wanted to get across to the reader. Your generosity and help has been overwhelming.

Introduction

If so many business leaders, experts, and researches all agree on the importance of trust to the bottom line and quality of life in the workplace, why does distrust continue to grow? In 2006, Steven M.R. Covey wrote a best-selling book called *The Speed of Trust, The One Thing That Changes Everything*. I couldn't agree more with the premise that fostering trust in the workplace would have a positive global impact on our economy and our lives. Business leaders around the globe have acknowledged trust is a key ingredient to success. Yet, despite the agreed-upon beneficial financial and social impact, more than a decade later trust in the workplace continues to rapidly diminish (Claveria 2019). Why does the business community continue to ignore the benefits of trust and connectedness in the workplace?

My answer is business owners are not experts in creating or changing the culture of the company, and culture is where trust resides. When trust becomes part of the corporate culture, everything changes for the better because all businesses have one thing in common—people. The term "employee" denotes some faceless cog in a machine. Businesses, your business, are made up of people who happen to work for you. These people, your staff, can no more separate out their personal issues and baggage from their work than you can separate out your soul from your body.

Henry Ford once asked, "Why is it every time I ask for a pair of hands, they come with a brain attached?" By all accounts Henry believed he was smarter and better than all of the people working for him. While Henry was probably smarter than each individual worker, he was not smarter or more creative than they were collectively. He also knew his workers would be easier to manage if they checked their brains at the factory entrance. What he didn't realize at the time, however, was he was asking his people to leave their passion, desire, and creativity behind. In today's world that type of thinking is no longer relevant or sustainable.

Why is this important to you? First, the business world is changing rapidly and businesses using the old corporate capitalism models are now being outpaced by the social capitalistic companies. The concepts of social capitalism have been written about for decades and have become integrated into businesses for the past two decades. For my purposes, the best definition of social capitalism I have found so far is:

> companies that strive through their words and deeds to endear themselves to all their primary stakeholders—customers, employees, suppliers, communities, and shareholders—by aligning the interests of all in such a way that no stakeholder group gains at the expense of other stakeholder groups; rather, they prosper together (Sisodia, Sheth and Wolfe 2014, p. xxiii)

Think of Starbucks, Whole Foods, Gore, and Hewlett-Packard (before Carly Fiorina) as businesses that have embraced this model. According to research over a 10-year period, the social capitalistic companies outperformed corporate capitalistic companies 1,026 percent to 331 percent a 3 to 1 ratio; (Sisodia, Sheth and Wolfe 2014, p. 15).

Second, I believe there will continue to be an ever-increasing demand for great talent. Companies who want to compete for the best and the brightest will have to be places that will attract upcoming generations of workers. World War II veterans are gone; us baby-boomers are phasing out of the workforce by the thousands every year. These older generations of workers are being replaced by Gen X, Gen Y, Millennials, Gen Z, and now Gen Alpha. Each new generation is becoming less tolerant of the more old school office environment. They want a sense of connectedness, collaboration, and appreciation. All of that depends on a foundation of trust. You want the best and the brightest working for you, create a place where they will come and stay. Otherwise, you may find yourself choosing from those that are left. Not an enviable position.

This book is designed to be a practical guide, resource, and workbook for CEOs, executives, managers, and employees to create a foundation of trust on which to build your corporate culture. I believe trust continues to decline in the workplace because there is no clear-cut way to create and sustain it. Instead, trust is assumed to exist as a matter of employment. This assumption leads to all manner of miscommunications, unrealized expectations, lost efficiencies, bad feelings, resentments, betrayals, and just about any other negative feeling you can imagine that obstructs the ability of your people to work together.

As one of my coaching colleagues recently pointed out, "our ability to connect with each other has withered to the point where many people prefer to text information or tweet their thoughts to avoid the pressure of a conversation." The 2019 *Edelman Trust Report* indicated only 37 percent of employees trusted the credibility of their CEO (Claveria 2019). How hard do you believe it will be to grow your business if almost two-thirds of the people doubt the leadership and they are afraid to talk to each other? Trust is the key to change all that.

Trust has been defined in countless ways over the years, as confidence, belief in someone or something, or integrity to name a few. However, I believe most definitions miss the mark and for the purposes of this book I define trust as: *the degree to which I am willing to be vulnerable: physically, emotionally, or financially vulnerable to another person(s)*. One big challenge in defining trust is that it is not logical; your emotions drive your desire to trust or distrust someone, not your intellect! None of us feel things the same way, so we lack the common reference points normally used to define a word. I'll use this example: try defining the color red to a person who has been blind since birth. There are no reference points this person could understand. That being said, one of the biggest mistakes we all make is assuming others intuitively understand what trust means to us.

Trust, however, is so much more than just a word; it goes to the core of your human existence. Your sense of trust is based on a tangled mix of beliefs and complex feelings. Those feelings are forged by personal experiences and memories of past successes and heartaches. Your definitions of trust are as personal to you as your own fingerprints and greatly impact your ability to lead your company.

Trust and vulnerability are symbiotic and directly proportional. Without vulnerability, trust cannot form; without trust, vulnerability will not increase and the bonds between people will remain weak and fragile. It is in the very act of exposing yourself to others, being vulnerable, that gives birth to a sense of trust. Trust goes hand in hand with feeling vulnerability and safe at the same time.

Now, why on earth would you want to be vulnerable in the workplace? Why would you want to risk embarrassment, judgment, or ridicule by being vulnerable to others? If you are a hired CEO, you could lose your position. If you own the business, you certainly don't want to appear weak as a leader. It is much safer to put on the "armor—the thoughts, emotions, and behaviors you use to protect yourself" (Brown 2018, 12). If you are not vulnerable, then you can't be hurt or your fear will not show. Unfortunately the very act of putting on armor limits your success. Here's why.

When the armor is on, emotions don't get in and your emotions don't get out. As people, we connect with each other on an emotional level first and then intellectually. When the armor is on, it is very difficult if not impossible for others to connect with you. The first real danger for a leader is that it is human nature to distrust that which we cannot connect with or understand. It is too risky for me to trust you when I don't know what is going on behind your armor. The second real danger is if I as an employee cannot emotionally connect with you, my desire to follow you will dry up relatively quickly, my passion for your company will be replaced with a sense of dutiful obligation, and if the right opportunity comes along I am out of the door.

The huge benefits of being coached as a business owner led me to becoming an executive coach so I could help others. Twenty years of coaching and 10 years of researching the subject of trust has taught me one thing: people still don't understand it. Colleges and MBA courses almost always cover ethics, what you are morally and legally obligated to do even when no one is watching. Understanding ethics does not provide insight into the connectedness trust creates between people that drive business!

Technology is helping businesses innovate and change at an unprecedented rate. Newer generations of people want a friendlier, connected work environment where they feel safe and appreciated. Trust can make all that happen. You have to decide if you want to be ahead of that curve or be left behind it.

In the first part of this book, I will go into the basic fundamentals of trust because you can't create or change something you don't understand. I'll cover:

- Why it is important to understand the emotions of the people who work for you

- How trust is formed between people
- Why being vulnerable is not a sign of weakness in a leader
- How trust in leadership creates phenomenal followers
- How past wounds can negatively impact current decisions
- How the connection between emotions and intellect forge great leaders

In the second part of this book, I will talk about the interaction between your people and trust in the workplace:

- How to set a foundation for future changes
- Why a solid organizational chart can help streamline a change in culture
- The acts that either kill or build trust between people
- The important differences between confidence, competence, and trust
- Creating tools for qualifying and quantifying trust in the workplace

In the last part of the book, I will go over a step-by-step process for creating a trusting environment where your people can thrive. You will have to make important decisions regarding:

- Whether to follow the path of social or corporate capitalism.
- What type of leader do you want to be?
- How to have very different more effective conversations in your business.
- The ability to sustain trust once it has been created.
- Trust in a virtual workforce.
- What's the next best version of your company?

Creating a culture of trust must start with you first, and from the top to the bottom of the organization. It will not work by telling employees to trust each other or expect it to happen organically. One of the basic tenants of trust is integrity. You must walk your talk by taking ownership of your thoughts, words, and deeds. As Ralph Waldo Emerson put it,

"Your actions speak so loudly I cannot hear what you say." Without this commitment on your part, any attempt at creating trust in the workplace will end very poorly.

One last piece about this book before you start, this work is not about theory or an academic exercise for me. It is very real, personal, and something I am passionate about. My work on this started from the almost knockout punches of my ex-wife leaving me for a younger man after 18 years of marriage, the betrayal of my wife and I by a close family member and the near financial ruin when a trusted business partner took my share of my business without paying for it.

People I trusted deeply turned out not to be trustworthy. I was hurt and embarrassed and vowed never to be hurt like that again. I armored up with the best defenses I could find. But my life and business didn't improve, because without some level of trust I had no connections with others. People didn't want to do business with me because they couldn't connect with me and they certainly didn't want to be around an unhappy person. I was no longer an effective leader. Fortunately, I was blessed to meet an incredible woman who has since become my wife. She helped me explore and understand the concepts I mentioned above. Through that journey came this book and doing the work that I love by connecting with others. I want to do the same for you.

Helping you understand trust is not enough because we are seeing distrust grow on a daily basis in commerce and industry. CEOs and top executives like you must be the standard bearers of trust, not just talk about it. This book is designed to help teach you how to be that example, and in doing so show employees how they too can help create trust where they work. It's up to you to do the work, the choice is yours.

PART I

A New Understanding of Trust

CHAPTER 1

Vulnerability and Trust

I always ask my clients to set a current benchmark before starting a new project and I suggest you do the same before reading further. The easiest way to do this is by journaling each time you read, or if possible on a daily basis. Start with a current assessment of your work environment. Do your people appear to be engaged with their work and connected to each other? Is everyone operating at peak performance or is there room for improvement? The more honest you are with your current assessment the better. Moving your business from point A to point B is much easier when both points are clearly defined. Your journaling should include what you are thinking and feeling after each chapter in the book. There are questions for reflection at the end of each chapter to help this process.

Another request I have for you is to read with as open a mind as possible. New coaching clients tend to have an urge to quickly dismiss ideas and thoughts they already know will not work or makes them feel uncomfortable. My experience has taught me, it is the very ideas you disagree with or make you uncomfortable, that create the nexus of change for you going forward.

Vulnerability Is Not Weakness

Trust and vulnerability are the flip side of the same coin and in order to create a trust based culture, you have to understand the nature of vulnerability. Being vulnerable is used frequently in the context of being weak, frail, fearful, and easily susceptible to attack or injury. That is one definition, but the opposite is true for creating trust. It takes great courage to become emotionally or physically vulnerable to another person(s).

I went to New York State Maritime College in the late seventies. It was at the end of the Vietnam War and returning veterans were not held in high regard. Several of these combat veterans attended school with us but didn't talk much about their experiences. They felt the general public wasn't interested in what they had to say. Fortunately, times have changed, veterans are now much more appreciated for their service and willing to write about what it is like to be a soldier under fire.

One recent book, *Extreme Ownership, How U.S. Navy Seals Lead and Win* by ex-Navy Seals Jocko Willink and Leif Babin stands out to me because the authors write about using military training to enhance business operations. The authors go into detail on how Seal training, planning, and debriefing after every mission can be used in business.

I bring this book up because I want you to visualize and create a mental image of these tough, fearless battle tested warriors working in your office. Being vulnerable to others in this environment would seem unlikely, however, their very success on the battlefield depended on their willingness to be completely vulnerable to their fellow squad members. Each Seal relied on the other to be ready, without hesitation, to give their life for each other. "I've got your back" takes on a whole new meaning when you're being shot at from all directions.

While this is an extreme example of complete vulnerability, imagine the impact that type of trust would have on your working relationships. This is the sense of trust and feeling safe that people want at work. They don't want to feel open or exposed and want to know that their co-workers will have their back. Who do you feel will be more productive, creative, innovative and industrious at work, someone who feels alone and afraid or a person who feels connected and safe?

This is one of the main reasons I believe trust is the key to unlocking success. Imagine for one moment what that type of personal connectedness could do to achieve your corporate goals? Or, as President Harry Truman once said, "It is amazing what you can accomplish if you do not care who gets credit."

Leaders and Followers

All leaders have two things in common, people who follow and their current situation. CEOs have workers and their everyday challenges. You cannot lead your followers if you don't understand what motivates them and how to clearly assess the challenges they face. You also face the challenge that no two people in your company are the same. Each one brings all of their personal experiences, biases, filters, and "baggage" to work every day. While it is impossible to understand all the underlying behavioral drivers there are certain common elements.

Fear is probably the most destructive motivator in the workplace. Fear of losing a job, being embarrassed, not being able to do the job, and most importantly the fear of not being physically or emotionally safe. Many laws have been passed in the last several decades to protect workers from physical, emotional, and verbal abuse. However, it saddens me to know that we have to pass legislation to create a safe place to work. But what impact does "safe space" really have on your business? Everything, and I will give you a few examples of emotional drivers you can't visibly see.

Safe Space

Part of my EMT training is to recognize and report sexual and emotional abuse to the proper authorities when we see it. Training has taught me that one in four women have reported being sexually abused. Women now make up over 50 percent of the workforce. If one in four have been abused that means at least 25 percent of the woman working for you right now have experienced this type of abuse. Imagine for a moment the impact this has on their working relationships?

Abuse of power in the workplace has reached epidemic proportions. Bill Cosby and Harvey Weinstein are just the tip of the iceberg in one highly visible industry. Women are finally coming out from behind their shame and demand to be heard "we will not tolerate this abuse of power anymore." The pent-up anger and frustration are now being released and it's why I believe the "#metoo" movement has caught on like wildfire. It will have long lasting and far-reaching impact on corporate cultures. The abuse of power and the fear it creates kills trust, demotivates workers and causes unnecessary lost productivity

I have been a "trusted advisor," executive coach, CEO peer group facilitator and business consultant for almost twenty years. I have had the honor and privilege of spending several thousand hours working with people to help them work through the tough issues they face in business and life. My clients are real people with moving stories and I will be using some of my client's stories (names and some details changed to protect their anonymity) to illustrate the points I want you to remember.

I'll share one story of abuse and fear from my client Elizabeth. She was a well-educated, articulate executive working her way up the corporate ladder in a large global company. What she didn't share was the fact that she had been date raped to near death as a younger woman. It took major surgery and several weeks in the hospital to physically recover, but the emotional scars still remained. One day she asked her boss a question about the course of action he was taking to manage a co-worker. Her question must have triggered something in him and he lost it. This six foot seven, 250 lb. man leaned over his desk, pointed his finger in her face and started screaming at her that she had no right to question his actions.

Elizabeth feared for her life, lost all sense of time and the control of her emotions. She was immediately transported to that rape long ago. She started shaking violently, became incontinent, ran out to her car crying and drove home. She was so scared and embarrassed over who might have witnessed this event, she was afraid to go back to work.

Imagine for a minute what her boss's single act did to her ability to work with him. Elizabeth came to me afraid to speak up for fear of reprisal from her boss. She shared her story and I helped her to create coping skills to keep her composure when not feeling safe. We also documented her case to take to her HR department and filed a complaint. Her boss was eventually let go, but the damage was already done. She no longer felt safe working for this company and left to find a better place to work. She has since gone on to become a vice president and thriving in her new company.

Abuse of trust is not limited to woman. The global cover up of sexual abuse of boys by Roman Catholic Church priests and scout leaders in the Boy Scouts, has shaken our sense of trust to its core. The men in these respected institutions were supposed to be role models of integrity and trust, yet these organizations covered up the abuse for decades. Men as well as women have been too embarrassed to come forward, until now, but their pain and suffering has been carried for a lifetime. Both woman and men want a safe space to work.

More people are being prescribed anti-anxiety medications than ever before to cope with stress. Global revenue is expected to reach close to

$17 billion annually for prescribed antidepressants. The negative impact on bottom-line profitability from poor performance, excessive time off, increased turnover and low morale causes businesses in the United States to lose over $210 billion annually (Sifferlin 2017). Every morning your people bring all of these issues with them as they walk through your doors.

Your work environment can ease much of those fears, reduce stress, and increase productivity (Vennie 2017). Some of the things I mention above are visible or self-evident others are not so visible. I'll bring up one way that your own organizational design possibly creates unnecessary stress. Roles and responsibilities are created to get your work done. What is missing is the authority and level at which each person can make decisions within those roles to get the work done before going to someone else for permission. I have found this one thing has a profound impact on stress levels, work efficiency, and trust. I'll go into more depth on this later in the book, it is that important.

Trust Is Not Psychological Safety

The concept and use of psychological safety is becoming much more prevalent in business, however while trust and psychological safety may appear to be the same, they are not. There is well-documented research that creates the following distinction. Psychological safety is experienced on a group level. Do your employees feel safe to express themselves, offer suggestions, or provide feedback without fear of rejection or retaliation? (Edmondson 2019, 17) Trust as I expressed earlier goes much deeper, it operates on a relationship level that depends on vulnerability.

At all levels in your business creating safe space through trust can make all the difference in reducing stress and anxiety. The next few sections are going to highlight some other subtle behaviors that decrease efficiency and diminish profitability.

Self-Sabotage—Not Trusting Yourself

I believe self-sabotage could actually be an Olympic event! Around the globe men and women train daily for just the right moment to score a perfect ten in foiling their own plans. This subject alone could keep me in business as an executive coach because it plagues most leaders and followers on a regular basis.

One of the most insidious forms of self-sabotage is holding back, not giving any task your very best for fear of publicly failing or being embarrassed if things don't go well. This form of self-sabotage shows up in different ways. One classic form of sabotage is perfectionism (Chamine 2012, 19). I've seen CEOs:

- Second guess themselves over and over again in an attempt to get it "just right."
- Not attempting something because they couldn't stand the criticism if it was not perfect right away.
- Not giving 100 percent effort because they couldn't live with the knowledge that they gave their best effort and still failed.

Is there anything you would have attempted in your life if there was absolutely no fear of embarrassment?

Perfectionism is only one of the many forms of self-sabotage that happens in your business every day. Research has shown people will sabotage their own efforts to bring them to the level of performance where they believe they should be (Shechtman 1998). One of the best examples of self-sabotage I know is the story of Roger Bannister.

Up until 1954 doctors and scientists believed it was impossible for a human being to run a mile in under four minutes. They said the runner's lungs would collapse and their heart would explode from the exertion. Roger refused to accept their theories believing he could break that barrier. He had no one to train with as no runner had done this before. He devised a plan to keep pace with the four best quarter mile runners he could find. He ran one lap around the track with each pace runner to keep up his speed. On May 6, 1954 he ran a mile in 3 minutes, 59.4 seconds and lived. It only took 46 days for the next runner to break his record. Runners no longer worried about their health in breaking the four-minute mile. Now they had a new goal of beating the last fastest time. Are there any self-limiting beliefs you believe to be true about your business?

This is another reason why creating safe space at work is so important. It allows your employees to be more vulnerable, and less inclined to hold back for fear of embarrassment or retaliation.

Self-Sabotage—Not Trusting Others

A CEO friend of mine referred me to an employee named Lilly. She was bright, educated, and well-spoken. She worked hard, but was struggling in her position. Even with all of her skills she had trouble working with others. This issue was affecting her overall performance and limiting her ability to be promoted.

Lilly preferred to work on her own because she always got her work done. Her team projects, however, never turned out well. Lilly blamed her co-workers for not keeping up with her, and the other employees complained of her lack of leadership. Her boss believed she just needed some work on her interpersonal skills, and sent her to me for coaching.

Executive coaching requires a high degree of trust between myself and the other person(s) involved. I have to create a safe space where my clients feel comfortable enough to share what was going on for them. There can be no judgment or assumptions, trust between people cannot be forced or coerced: it evolves.

Lilly was hesitant to discuss her workplace challenges. She was hurt, upset, and angry at being singled out for "coaching." She viewed the coaching as punishment and wanted to "fix" whatever the problem was so she could get back to work. I assured her I didn't assume she was "broken," so there was no need to "fix" her.

Business owners tend to be "fixers," identify the problem and fix it so you can move on. Digging into issues quickly usually results in symptoms being corrected but not the underlying causes. It works the same way with people. Dig into them too quickly and the armor goes on. I usually start by talking about subjects that are considered safe—where you grew up, what were your parents and siblings like, hobbies, and so on. Topics that don't require a lot of vulnerability to share. This breaks the ice and builds some rapport. Creating safe space is more important than quickly digging into the possible reasons why Lilly's team projects didn't go well.

Small talk was difficult for Lilly, she wanted to get on with whatever needed to be done so she could go back to work. I asked her how long it would take her to realize that doing things the same way would not yield different results. Rational thinking was important to Lilly and that message got through. She got it and decided it was in her best interest to work with me than be angry about it.

Lilly shared that she grew up in a household where her father worked three jobs and was rarely home. Her mother was a perfectionist who wanted everything in the house, including the children, to be perfect. Her mom's expressions of love came in the form of perpetual criticism. Everything could be better, and personal choice was nonexistent. Her father didn't realize the effect his wife's critical comments were having on the kids. He was just too tired after working all day to notice. Lilly grew up desperately trying to be perfect to avoid her mother's criticism and gain her father's affection. As a result, the adult Lilly had little patience for those who were not up to speed. She didn't feel emotionally safe anywhere and kept her feelings to herself. Putting on her armor made life easier for herself but very difficult for those around her to connect with her.

Lilly didn't realize she had a real distrust of people and their feelings, or the importance of connecting with others to work effectively. In her mind she didn't need relationships to get ahead—she felt she could do it on her own. All she had to do was get her education, work hard, stay focused and all would be well. She didn't need input from others and was quick to judge them. What Lilly failed to grasp is even a one-person business still requires building relationships even if it is only with clients and vendors. Her current beliefs about trust and relationships were causing major self-sabotage to her career.

Lilly had an internal battle going on, even when complimented by others she was always waiting for the criticism to follow. Criticism was a way of life for her. She was so predisposed to it she was extremely sensitive to any hint of negativity in conversation.

A Turning Point

For Lilly, the first step was for her to acknowledge that her current beliefs were a form of self-sabotage and holding her back. This was a tough for her, it meant she wasn't perfect. But Lilly was exhausted from being at odds with her co-workers and didn't know what to do about it. Once she became aware of her self-sabotaging beliefs, the next crucial step was to break this cycle. Criticism and distrust had become a way of life for her and familiarity makes you feel safe.

To break the cycle she had to stop making assumptions about other people and situations. I showed her how judgment shuts down discernment and critical thinking! I'll talk more about that later. Her fear of not having the answer forced her to make assumptions instead of asking questions. Asking great questions is an incredibly powerful tool for building relationships and connecting with others. Lilly and I turned her "know it all" mentality into asking thoughtful questions instead. She no longer needed to be right to protect her ego.

It took time for Lilly to break this habit and lower her armor. Connecting with co-workers was still awkward at first, but once they realized she was sincere in her efforts they warmed up to her. Once she started connecting she saw the very noticeable positive results from her team projects and she no longer feared not having the answer. Now, instead of being criticized, she has been commended for making others on her team feel important and empowered. Her team has now become the role model for others in her company.

Self-Deception and Trust

Self-deception are the lies you tell yourself or the justifications you use when a choice you make goes against your internal core values. Sometimes the deception is consciously made and other times you don't even realize you are doing it (The Arbinger Institute 2010). Either way it is still a form of self-sabotage and can become an unconscious habit of lying to yourself. I know, I used to do it, a lot.

Years ago I was going through a very rough time. I had decided to merge my existing business in with another firm. Within a short time I realized the other business owner had very low standards for personal values and ethics. Even after I knew I had made a very bad choice I kept telling myself I could make it work. Well, I was dead wrong and I couldn't believe what happened next. I had just returned from Florida after visiting with my dad who was dying of lung cancer. I barely got in the door when he accused me of unethical behavior and forced me out of the business.

He cut off my paycheck and kept all the clients I had brought with me without paying for them. Overnight, I found myself out on the street, working as a hired CEO and doing overnight shifts as an EMT to keep the roof over my family's head and food on our table. I had been lying to myself to justify the poor choice I had made in trusting the wrong person. That choice cost me and my family years of hard work and a lot of money, or as my daughter put it "we were broke but not broken."

Ultimately, I had to confront the facts. I didn't do enough research into the character of the person or the ethics in his business dealings. It was tough to swallow but I channeled my anger into the impetus to put pen to paper and write about trust. I share this because I believe none of us are immune from lying to ourselves to avoid taking ownership of poor choices. You lose your integrity by not admitting your mistakes and make a better decision to correct it. This topic is so important I will bring it up time and time again in this book. The ability to move beyond self-deception and justification will help create a platform for creating an environment of trust and connect all your stakeholders.

Thoughts for Reflection

- How do you feel about being vulnerable to others?
- Take a mental inventory of where you may have self-sabotaged your efforts in your life. Are there times or places you still hold back from your best effort?
- How do you talk to yourself when you have made a mistake? Are you harshly critical and continually punishing yourself long after the mistake was made?
- Have you found yourself blaming others for poor results in order to justify the choices you made?
- Do you feel more comfortable leading or following?
- Do you consider following being weak?
- Have you ever regretted not speaking up for yourself when you had the chance?

Please add more in your own journal.

CHAPTER 2

Priming Yourself to Trust

I became interested in neuro-linguistic programming back in the 1980s when I left the merchant marine and got into sales. I wanted to learn how to connect with people as part of my sales process rather than use a canned speech. Many years later when I became an executive coach I started reading different books on neuroscience in an effort to connect on a deeper level with my clients. In 2010 I met one speaker on this subject, Judith E. Glaser, who caught my attention because she spoke directly about the power of words and human connections. She published *Conversational Intelligence, How Great Leaders Build Trust and Get Extraordinary Results* (Glaser 2014) in 2016, and I spent the following year with Judith and her team becoming certified in Conversational Intelligence® to better understand the neuroscience behind effective conversations.

Priming for Trust

It's worth bringing in some of the neurochemistry at this point to help you understand what goes on internally when your senses are triggered. Science has proven that all the cells in your body are wired to pick up and resonate with your emotions. And here's why.

There are thousands upon thousands of neuro-receptors in each cell of your bodies. Each receptor is tied to one specific peptide (a protein chemical). Each feeling of anger, joy, sadness, love, guilt, excitement, happiness, nervousness, and so on releases its own flood of neuropeptides (chemicals) instantly into your body. Those peptides connect with the specific receptors in each cell, changing the structure of the cell as a whole. Think of it as little light switches being turned up (positive) and down (negative) in each cell.

When you perceive something as negative, that switch is flipped to the down negative position and depression-inducing chemicals (cortisol, testosterone) are released and penetrate all your cells within seconds. If the perception is positive, then the switch is flipped up and your system releases the "feel good" chemical oxytocin creating a natural high (Grodnitzky 2014, 11).

Judith E. Glaser calls the positive release sequence "priming for trust" (Glaser 2014, 107). I look at it as carefully starting to take your protective armor off. It is also important to understand the future impact of flipping those switches up and down over time. When your body cells are exposed to negative chemicals more than positive ones you flip the switch down more than up, each new cell produced by those cells are already programmed to be negative. Here is where the power of conversation in creating trust comes in.

Starting a New Conversation

Words in and of themselves do not have power, that is created by the emotions we associate with those words. I am a firm believer that "The pen is mightier than the sword" (Bulwer-Lytton 1839) in that communication (written and verbal) is a far more effective way to get people to do what you ask willingly rather than through fear and violence.

You have two basic forms of conversations, the ones you have with others and the ones you have with yourself. I'm focusing on the negative self-talk for the moment because with each negative thought you are literally programming your cells to be more negative in the future. Over time, negativity becomes a familiar feeling and remember, you feel safe with feelings that are familiar. It doesn't mean that is healthy for you, your mind doesn't know the difference. It just wants to be safe now and is not interested in the future impact. Would you say you have more positive conversations with yourself or negative ones? Which ones help and which conversations hold you back?

This programming now carries over into your external conversations with unexpected implications. More and more conversations today are replaced by texting, tweeting, Instagram, Snapchat, Facebook posts and other nonverbal communications. Why? Because it is easier to feel safe behind electronic walls rather than have a face to face conversations. Being in front of another person exposes you, you may not feel safe and it becomes stressful. I work with people who struggle to express themselves and avoid important conversations. They are more willing to suffer silently than risk conflict or damage a relationship by talking. The sad part is, not having that conversation actually weakens the relationship instead of protecting it (Scott 2002, 6).

The last important thing to remember from this chapter is that your thoughts, your internal conversation will literally program your mind to receive more of what you think about. It is the science behind the famous turn of the century book *Think and Grow Rich* by Napoleon Hill. He chronicled from observation and conversations with highly successful individuals the power of positive self-talk long before the body chemistry part was understood. It takes more than a few positive thoughts to make a significant impact on your long-term mental state. Every cell in your body is replaced every two months. It takes a fair amount of time to turn years of negative priming around in your body. To do this you have to consciously catch your negative self-talk and focus more on the lesson to be learned than the self-recrimination. Be patient, it takes time and it works.

Thoughts for Reflection

- Have you ever caught yourself putting down or gossiping about someone in order to make yourself feel better?
- Are your internal conversations generally positive or negative?
- Do you understand that mentally saying positive things is not the same as embracing positive thoughts?
- How cognizant are you of the words you use? Are they chosen careful or do you just say what is on your mind?
- Do you understand why leaders cannot make loose or idle comments?
- Do people generally feel more positive or negative after talking with you?

CHAPTER 3

Is Trust Given or Earned?

The giving and receiving of trust is probably one of the most precious interactions between you and another person. Understanding this dynamic is crucial for trust to be accepted with the same reverence it is offered.

I was talking to my friend Keith about a few of the challenges he faced with his staff. The floor managers reporting to him didn't work well together. One manager would come to him complaining about another rather than talking directly to that person. He said the level of distrust on the production floor was causing unnecessary friction, production delays, upsetting clients and inhibiting Keith's efforts to streamline the production process.

Keith is a production expert and hired to fix the manufacturing issues the CEO knew he was having but didn't know what was causing them. Keith had no idea when he arrived how toxic the culture on the production floor had been for years. As an expert Keith knows changing a process can often mean changing people and there were several he wanted to let go. The CEO however was hesitant to fire anyone because the plant was located in a rural town with a small employee pool to choose from.

Our conversation about the distrust between co-workers and with the management, slowly morphed into a discussion about the deeper meaning of trust and the "which came first, the chicken or egg" question of "Is trust given or is it earned?" Keith said without hesitation "You have to earn my trust before I'm willing to give it to you."

I thought about this for a moment and asked him, "What would it take for me to earn your trust?"

He responded, "I am not absolutely sure but I will know when it happens."

I told him I don't read minds well, "If you can't tell me, how am I supposed to know?"

Keith looked pained as said "Come on Russ, you're a smart guy, you know what it takes to earn someone's trust."

Pushing even further, I asked, "Would you be able to write down a list of what I have to do to earn your trust so I don't have to make assumptions?"

"Probably not," Keith replied.

"Even if you could create a list, do you think it would ever be complete?" I asked.

"I doubt it," he said again.

Giving and Earning Trust

The late Jack Welch, former CEO of GE was asked for his definition of trust, Jack said "You know it when you feel it" (Covey 2008, p. 5). His answer gives me no insight into his thinking because no two people are going to feel or describe trust the same way. I ask clients "Is trust earned or given?" when trust issues in a relationship are apparent. The overwhelming response is that trust needs to be earned. Earning trust is a misnomer, I have to be trustworthy in another person's viewpoint before they will give me their trust. I may believe I am trustworthy, but until the other person agrees their trust will be withheld. All my years of working with others has taught me this misconception about giving and earning trust has created countless misunderstandings, hurt feelings, and broken relationships.

Remember, your concept of trust is very personal and more emotional than logical. Have you ever felt uneasy or distrustful of someone who doesn't feel the same way you do about politics, religion, disciplining children, money, or even pets? I remember hearing one individual at civic meeting say "I could never trust someone who doesn't like dogs, they're just not nice people!" I know it sounds shallow and judgmental, but that thinking goes on inside many people all the time.

Creating Your List

If you want some insight into your own feelings, create your own personal list of what it would take for me to earn your trust using the format in

Table 3.1 below. Write down any words, actions, or movements (even tone of voice, body language, facial hair, tattoos, etc.) that provoke feelings of "safe" or "unsafe."

Table 3.1 Safe–Unsafe Table

What Makes Me Feel Safe?	What Makes Me Feel Unsafe?
People who tell the truth.	People who gossip or talk about others behind their backs.
People who listen to me when I speak.	People who talk at me or over me and don't listen.
People who have a genuine smile.	People who smile only when they want something from me.
People who return things that do not belong to them.	People who steal or take what is not theirs.
People who respect me.	People who are rude to me or others around me.
Being surrounded by people I know or in familiar surroundings.	Being around strangers or in unfamiliar places.
People who love pets.	People who abuse animals.
People who respectfully offer their opinions.	People who constantly judge others or are confrontational.
People who encourage and help those not as strong mentally, physically, or emotionally as they are.	People who are bullies.
People who are vulnerable with me.	People who are emotionally closed off.
People who look me in the eyes when speaking to me.	People who always look away when talking to me.
Add your own.	

Be brutally honest with yourself here. The safe list could include skin color, religion, politics, hobbies, right down to who loves dogs. The unsafe list could simply be the opposite of those things—different skin color or religion, or loves cats but not dogs (dog lover is on my safe list). I want to increase your awareness about things that makes you feel one way or the other. It could be past experiences or social conditioning. It doesn't matter what the back story is, just write it down. List them side by side as I have done in the table and save your list for future reference. You will need this for creating an environment of trust with your staff and they will have their own lists as well.

Understand, that even if another person appears to do everything on your "safe" list, it does not mean you must automatically trust them! The choice to give your trust must be a conscious one made for the appropriate reasons. Too many people place their need for connectedness over discerning first if the other person(s) is trustworthy. Don't rush and also don't be silent about the depth of trust you want in your relationship. Personal power comes from clarity on what behavior you will and will not accept in your life.

Familiarity Makes You Feel Safe

Recognizing patterns is one of your body's oldest early warning systems, is this person or situation safe or dangerous? Can I be hurt or die? Can I trust them or not? In his international bestseller, *Thinking, Fast and Slow*, Daniel Kahneman, the renowned psychologist and winner of the Nobel Prize in Economics, describes how the amygdala (the little walnut-sized part of our brain) is incredibly efficient at pattern recognition. As you see a pattern start to unfold, you quickly determine if the pattern is unleashing something that can hurt you or that you can trust. Every day, all day long, we are constantly assessing people and situations to remain safe. Later in the book I will show you how to change patterns or conversations that may be sending out the wrong message.

Pattern recognition comes in the form of things people do to or for us. It can be a series of small gestures or larger more pronounced acts (Brown 2018, p. 32). On some level, you keep the plus and minus scores in your mind for the people you know. A check goes in the plus column each time someone is supportive, compassionate, or keeps your secrets, and so on. A minus is given when they gossip about you, are disrespectful, mean or negative in some other way.

Employees notice patterns of behavior in you, co-workers, vendors, and clients. They do it without even thinking, and judge what they hear or see. Patterns of integrity, honesty, and trustworthiness go in the plus column while patterns of manipulation, lying, pandering, and dishonesty go on the minus side.

Another very important pattern for discussion in this section revolves around employee concepts of fairness. The topic of being fair comes up over and over again for debate in the CEO groups I run. Employees do not equate fairness with how management is treating them, but how they feel management is treating everyone else around them. Employees instantly recognize perceived patterns of personal favoritism, special treatment of certain people of divisions and C-Suite executives taking care of themselves while the staff suffers. These perceptions are reinforced by assumptions and gossip in the informal networks and are toxic in any company.

Plus and minus patterns can show up in the formal and informal communications and behaviors within your company. The formal part resides in company policies and procedures, how we are supposed to do things. The informal side is what employees observe and emulate in "how we really do things around here." This includes inside politics, gossip, power plays, and all the other dramas that occur whenever a group of people are put together. The greater the gap between the formal and the informal communications will determine the degree of integrity and trust felt within your company. The closer the alignment, the higher the trust.

In 2016 the financial world was rocked by the news that employees of the esteemed 165-year-old Wells Fargo Bank had been opening accounts in clients' names without those clients' consent or knowledge. According to the Consumer Financial Protection Bureau, "employees opened more than 2 million unauthorized accounts, sticking customers with almost $2.5 million in fees." The author also notes Wells Fargo "had a 37-page 'Vision and Values' brochure that explains, at length, how the bank puts its customers first. The document uses the word 'trust' 24 times" (Staley 2016). At the time, Wells Fargo was the 4th largest bank in the world. Thirty-seven pages of written values had little impact on preventing managers and employees from being pressured to cross-sell accounts, get the numbers up or else. As many as 5,300 employees lost their jobs over this and Wells Fargo is still trying to regain trust in the marketplace. The gap between the formal and informal communication was as wide as the Grand Canyon.

How Others See You

Next, I want you to focus on the conscious patterns you can create in your thoughts, words, and deeds that will allow others to feel they can trust you. Remember, as quickly as you are sizing up another person, they are doing the same to you! They too have their own "safe/unsafe" list and you can't control what is on it. Trying to get them to trust you generally has the opposite effect. You can't be all things to all people, so stop trying. Just be trustworthy.

So, what does that really mean? Most people want to feel that they are trustworthy. I mean, who doesn't? Let me ask you, have you ever:

- Lied? Even "little white lies"? Over time lots of little lies will slowly erode the feeling of being safe. It gets others thinking, "If this person can so easily tell small lies, what else they are lying about?"
- Misused personal or positional power as the CEO or manager?
- Blamed others for failures that ultimately were your responsibility?
- Left out or omitted important facts from a report because it would reflect poorly on you?
- Found yourself gossiping about others (especially to feel important or to fit into a group)?
- Cheated, bent or changed the rules to suit your own needs?
- Taken what is not yours (including using office staff for your personal life tasks)?
- Had unrestricted emotions (being a "hot head," volatile, or uneven-tempered and taken it out on others)?
- Tried to manipulate someone's feelings to get them to like (or possibly love) you?
- Been guilty of self-centered or narcissistic behavior while not paying attention to others?
- Been condescending in your tone of voice, menacing, or—even worse—bullying those weaker than you?
- Expressed racial or religious prejudices (even in just telling a joke)?

Little White Lies

Being trustworthy means you must decide what you will and will not accept in your own behavior. Are little white lies told to protect others' feelings acceptable? The broader the range in your definition of what is acceptable, the harder it becomes for you to draw a line in the sand on what it means to be trustworthy. Everything becomes a "gray" area and ambiguity makes most people uneasy. That leads to not feeling safe and distrust sets in.

I will use an example of little white lies to show how you can change perspective, become more honest in your expressions, compassionate with others' feelings, and build trust. Some may argue that you should just express your "truth" without worrying about how it is received. Your "truth" however is not fact, it is only your opinion being expressed as a fact and that's judgment, not "truth." Being trustworthy requires discipline and mindfulness in your interactions with others—not just bulldozing over them because you are speaking your truth.

The assumptions behind telling white lies are these:

- First Assumption—You have made a judgment about someone or a situation that you know to be "the truth."
- Second Assumption—You believe that what you want to say will probably hurt them.
- Third Assumption—Your relationship with that person is not strong enough to withstand the pain your comments will create and causing irreparable damage to your relationship.
- Last Assumption—It is better to lie than hurt someone else.

I will use the classic question, "How do I look in this?" to dig deeper into the cost of little white lies in relationships. This question has been the subject of countless jokes and cartoons and, yet, it can be a real minefield in a relationship! Both parties should use caution and not look for a "safe" way to ask or avoid answering this question, since body image is a huge issue for so many people.

Here are the four assumptions for this question:

- First you judge what they are wearing either looks good or that the clothes don't fit well, are the wrong style or not appropriate for the event.

- If you don't like what they are wearing, you are not going to hurt their feelings by saying so. Instead you play it safe and say "You look great!"
- It is not worth the repercussions in your relationship to tell them what you are really thinking.
- The little white lie allows you to move past the awkward moment without any real discussion.

These scenarios of little lies and avoidance can go on forever. The point is, in order to maintain the integrity of trust, a different type of conversation should take place long before the, "How do I look in this?" question even comes up.

My wife and I are no less human than any other couple. It is a second marriage for both of us and we learned some valuable lessons in our prior relationships. My wife still changes her mind about what to wear several times before she is satisfied with her appearance. Sometimes she will ask me what I think about her outfit, other times she will not. She knows I will give her an honest answer as to what I believe looks great on her. At the same time I also ask her about what to wear because I trust her sense of style more than my own. This works for us because everything said is done with respect and awareness about how sensitive the other person may be feeling about their appearance. This is the trust and intimacy we share as a couple.

This might all sound a bit shallow or simple. Telling "little white lies" all the time rather than risking hurt feeling is very socially acceptable. However, I offer this for your consideration. "Practice makes perfect" is an old saying. If you want to become great at any skill you must practice it over and over again. There are many who have become experts at telling "little white lies" because they have practiced them thousands of times. For some lying has become an art form, making it very difficult to know when they are telling us what they really think.

There is also the danger of "little white lies" becoming more complex and compounded, as one lie has to be told to cover the first lie, a second, the third, and a fourth lie—until the truth is obscured. Half-truths and important omissions also fall into this category. If you have ever been on the wrong end of these lies and half-truths, then you know how painful it can be.

What about "helpful" white lies in difficult situations? Doctors shielding patients from bad news, flight attendants assuring passengers it's "only turbulence" when it could be mechanical failure, and governments withholding information fearing mass public panic if the real news got out—these are just a few examples. Each leader must decide in the moment what is the appropriate thing to do. But before you do, go back and look closely at the assumptions you are making about the situation and the other people involved. Choose carefully!

As an EMT, I have been trained not to tell a patient in the back of an ambulance that they are going to be alright. I can't guarantee they will be fine, and lying to them about their condition will not help them. Instead, it is my responsibility to assure them we will get them to the hospital as quickly and safely as possible and keep them stable and comfortable as best as we can in the back of a moving vehicle. The fear in their eyes can create an overwhelming desire for any of the first responders to say they will be fine. But we can't risk breaking their trust for a short-lived "feel good" moment.

Un-learning the urge to say something we perceive to be "safe" is not easy. It takes time. So, pause, think, and take the time to respond with how you feel or what you are thinking with intention rather than defaulting to a lie, omission or avoiding the subject by responding "yes, dear." It is in these conversations that you can deepen the bonds of trust between you and others rather than fearing of damaging them.

Thoughts for Reflection

- How often do you tell "little white lies" to avoid expressing what you are feeling and thinking? Has it become second nature to tell them?
- How quick are you to judge and make assumptions about others?
- Take a fierce moral inventory of the bullet points mentioned about being trustworthy and the telling of little white lies

in this chapter, rate each point on a scale of 1 to 10, 1 being never and 10 being always.

- Do you default to trusting quickly or are generally distrustful of others?
- How does this concept of giving or earning trust show up for you with your direct reports, managers, or co-workers?
- Are you clear with others about your expectations on being trustworthy?

CHAPTER 4

Betrayal, Forgiveness, and Release

Stories of betrayal have existed since people first walked the face of the earth. History is full of monstrous betrayals of trust, causing countless acts of physical violence, emotional distress, suicide, murders, even wars. The reasons for those betrayals are as varied and complex as those involved. Being betrayed on any level hurts; the greater the vulnerability exploited, the deeper the pain. When Shakespeare penned "Et tu, Brute" in his play *Julius Caesar*, he wasn't describing a small indiscretion of dishonesty!

Feeling betrayed can tear at your soul and, if not addressed, can lead to depression and even suicide. I didn't truly grasp these feelings until I found out my ex-wife was having an affair with a co-worker. I felt humiliated (because it seems others already knew), violated, sick, angry, and trying to understand what I had done to be treated this way. I'm certainly not perfect but at least I felt more worthy of more respect than I received from a spouse. This episode in my life led me to discover the power of forgiveness and release.

First, it is extremely important for you to understand my definition of forgiveness in the context of this book. Forgiveness is not about accepting or condoning the acts of others. It is not about forgetting, "sucking it up," moving on, or any other clichéd term used to help someone "move on." Forgiveness is not about the other person(s) at all. It is about you.

Forgiveness is the process of letting go of your emotions surrounding the betrayal and not allowing those emotions to control you. Forgiveness starts by forgiving yourself for trusting the person who hurt you in the first place. Of course, telling you to let go of emotions is easier said than done. All too often, it is those very emotions you believe will keep you safe from future betrayals. However, the internal emotional damage you incur over time will be far worse than the next possible betrayal.

Personal Stories

While researching this subject for the book I reached out to my circle of business professionals, coaches, and former clients. I asked them to share their stories of betrayal and forgiveness to use in this book rather than citing stories others had written about. I expected the usual stories of lying, cheating, taking credit for others' work, passed over for promotion, and similarly related business stories. I had no idea what was going to happen next.

There were some stories like those mentioned above; however, some of the stories that came back were just overwhelming. I could not believe business people and professionals silently carried around so much pain and suffering. I had unintentionally opened a real can of worms with this subject! Some stories made me cry, other stories made me sad or just down right angry. In the end I am truly honored and humbled by the vulnerability these people shared with me. A few of the stories were just too gut-wrenching for this book; the stories below are intense and I included them to give real gravity to the subject.

- One executive shared her story of ultimately caring for the father who had sexually abused her as a child until he died. Her forgiveness of him at the end released decades of pain, guilt, and shame of what she had not told anyone.
- Another colleague shared that he no longer talked to his only sibling over the betrayal in handling their mother's affairs. She changed the will and left him out of it because she felt their parents had already "given him enough." He says he has forgiven but not forgotten.
- One executive shared how she had been humiliated and shamed in the school locker room because someone had taken a compromising photo and posted it on her locker. She still doesn't like using public bathrooms or showers.
- Another executive shared he had hid his dyslexia from others for years out of embarrassment and shame of not being able to read well and how foolish he felt when he did share and everyone bent over backwards to help him.

One fellow coach wrote back to me with her story and a big thank you for helping her realize that she was not as healed as she thought she was after years of inner work. She was so succinct in her writing I wanted to quote her rather than paraphrase her thoughts.

Hi Russ, wow, reading your draft chapter on betrayal hit me like a bolt of lightning! I wanted to put the book down and avoid it like the plague. Run, actually! My heart sped up and my throat felt dry and closed. I didn't run. I journaled. Then I did a healing on myself. I feel better and have continued to read. I have worked on myself forever, and self-awareness is key to growth. Therapy, Al-Anon's 12 steps, coaching and so on have been my primary tools for change. I grew up with an alcoholic father and a depression-filled mother. My father sexually abused me and my mom hid it for fear of being beaten. I was betrayed by both parents at a very young age. Trust was not a feeling I understood or knew how or whom or when to use it. I mostly didn't trust myself. This took decades to sort out with much help, but by then the untrustworthy list of folks in my life grew. Not that I knew if I was either, but knowing my level of responsibility both given and taken, it likely was a great deal of the time. I know that I have broken trust in my life and own it. I learn from my mistakes and amend the behavior along with an apology. Forgiveness is key to my peace of mind and allows me to be honest with myself when I have a "miss take" of word or act that needs amending. If I am fortunate, I may get another chance. This is the beginning of rebuilding trust that was lost. I have stronger boundaries with those who I am best keeping some distance from. Most important is that I want to be trustworthy and wish to honor others by trusting them at some level from the beginning. I am far from perfect and only look for personal progress as I work on being my best version of myself today. One day at a time. Russ, know that your words elicited this new thought about trust that helped me greatly, even though it truly scared me. I have worked on trust many times and had hoped I was good to go. Apparently not quite ;) Thank you.

After reading all of the stories sent back to me, I knew many others agreed upon the high importance of this subject. All of the people who shared their stories are experienced business owners, community leaders, and executive coaches. No matter how much they had accomplished in their professional lives, the inner person was still wounded. I knew from my own past experience that these wounds impacted my decision making, professional and personal relationships, and therefore my ability to lead.

Remember, the wounds of betrayal and other past hurts cloud the lens you filter everything through. As a CEO and leader, the clearer your lens, the easier it becomes to see people and situations as they are, not as they appear to be in your lens. To clean your lens, you must first be aware of what may be clouding it. Next are some steps on where and how to polish your lens.

Helpful Building Blocks

Awareness and Taking Ownership

There are at least two sides to every story of something that happened that may have caused you pain. The default position of most stories is to blame others for the pain that was caused by their actions. That's a victim mentality and kills your ability to lead. Instead, start off each story by asking yourself, "What part did I play in that story? What did I say or do that may have contributed to that outcome?" Placing blame first on others clouds the true nature of the story. Self-deception takes hold when you fail to take ownership of the choices you made. Admitting you may have made a mistake or contributed to the poor outcome is the proper step for polishing that story off your lens. Can you find other places that need to be polished off by taking ownership of the situation? These steps will become critical in helping others in your organization do the same when mistakes are made.

Forgiveness

Meaningful trust cannot exist in relationships without the forgiveness of past transgressions. There will always be lingering doubt: if I trust them again, am I opening myself up to more pain in the future? There are no guarantees because we all make mistakes. However, there is a lot you can do with forgiveness to improve your odds.

Forgiveness is one of the toughest and most non-negotiable requirements in trust. Please remember forgiveness is not about accepting or condoning the acts of others. It is about breaking the connection between memory and pain. Painful memories become ingrained in your mind because when trust is violated, the feelings release huge amounts of negative chemicals (cortisol, testosterone) into your system. Remember the switches in your cells I mentioned earlier? They all get flipped downwards in an instant. Each time those memories are triggered these same toxic chemicals in your system make you feel the pain all over again as if it were happening for the first time. That pain locks you in time to that moment similar to the movie *Groundhog Day* where the main character relives the same day over and over again. Forgiveness helps prevent those memories from being triggered, allowing you to move on from that point in time. Forgiveness breaks the associated pain with that memory and prevents the toxic chemicals from being released. That pain is left in the past and that memory is just a lesson to learn from.

Trust through Forgiveness

There are far too many paths to forgiveness to write down in this book. For some, forgiveness comes from their faith and religious teachings. It is a basic theme throughout most world religions: that not forgiving hurts you and separates you from the world, rather than hurting the other person.

When possible, I find it very helpful to engage the help of others in the forgiveness process. The very act of being vulnerable to someone and share the pain can start the healing process. Again, vulnerability is not a weakness: just the opposite, it takes strength and courage to engage others in this process.

I will share one resource I found helpful in writing this section. *Forgive for Good* by Dr. Fred Luskin is a great book for digging much deeper into this subject and understanding the impact that forgiveness has on your life. His writing is clear and concise and creates a solid framework for forgiving and moving on. At the end of his book he lists his Nine Steps for Forgiveness. I love the first line of his step number eight: "Remember that a life well-lived is your best revenge."

There are real dangers to not forgiving, physical and mental. The longer it takes, the more you start to identify yourself as either the betrayed (the victim) or the betrayer (the guilty). As long as you are the victim, you give away your personal power forever to the person(s) who betrayed us. And as the betrayer, you live in a state of guilt, shame, and embarrassment.

When you don't forgive, you refresh your anger and pain when the memory comes up—and it will come up. Those feelings cloud your lens each time. Your brain does not like unresolved issues and will constantly play the events over and over again trying to arrive at some type of resolution.

One final short story to illustrate the point of letting go. There are two monks on a pilgrimage to their holy monastery about two weeks away on foot. They have taken a vow of silence until they reach the monastery and a permanent vow of chastity. They are not allowed to look at or touch a woman.

They are three days into their journey when they come up to a young woman standing by the edge of a fast moving stream. She implores the monks to carry her across so she doesn't drown. The first monk bows politely and crosses the river. The second monk puts the young woman on his back, crosses the stream, and puts her down. She thanks him, he bows, and the two monks continue on their way.

They finally reach the monastery and are about to enter in when the first monk turns to the second monk and exclaims, "How can you possibly enter into the monastery! You touched a woman and broke your vow!" The second monk says, "I picked up that young woman and put her down in fifteen minutes, you have been carrying her for over a week and still do. My transgression was short lived. How long will yours last?" Is there anyone you are still carrying?

The point is the act of forgiveness must be a conscious choice; there must be a total surrendering of the negative feelings. There is no negotiating in surrender. Once your negative thoughts are released, you can replace them with positive ones and keep the lens clear.

Working Together

My grandfather once said, "When someone shows you their true colors, believe them." Most of us have the natural inclination of not trusting someone, once that trust is broken. That may not always be so easy to do when it involves your boss, a co-worker, or a person who reports to you. You may have to be in relationship with them in order to get your work done. There is no hard and fast rule that says you must repair a relationship; however, it may be in everyone's best interest to do so. Go back to taking ownership of the situation, what part did you play in that situation, and what can you do to prevent it from happening again? Here is where learning how to express yourself without blaming the other person can go a long way in mending fences.

Mindfulness

Once trust is broken, the relationship is no longer the same, nor would you want it to be. It was probably the structure of the old relationship that allowed for the trust to be broken in the first place. Rebuilding a working relationship requires mindfulness: being aware of how you are feeling and how those feelings are directing your actions. If your intention is to create a better relationship then a good outcome will usually follow.

Safe Boundaries

Improving the odds of building long-lasting, meaningful trust requires a change in your concept of boundaries (what you will and will not tolerate), the willingness to express your thoughts, the ability to listen to others, and the courage to "risk" your relationship in order to make it stronger. The depth and meaningfulness of your relationship is only confined by your willingness to trust the other person. This trust is established by the thoughts, words, and deeds that occur within the boundaries of the relationship. The process of rebuilding trust requires careful thought, reflection, and conversations around each of these building blocks. So take your time and allow each one of these subjects to sink in.

When You Are the Betrayer

What happens when you are the one on the other side of the broken trust equation? I am going to make the assumption that, at some point in time, you have broken or betrayed someone's trust. From the simplest of lies to the deepest forms of abuse, we all make mistakes. It is one of the bonds that make us human. I have a quote from Dale E. Turner over my desk that says,

> It is the highest form of self-respect to admit your errors and mistakes and make amends for them. To make a mistake is only an error in judgment, but to adhere to it when it is discovered shows infirmity of character.

Owning and acknowledging one's mistakes helps you to learn from them and to use those lessons to create better future outcomes. You may have felt justified in your actions because they perpetrated some act against you; "the ends justified the means" so to speak. However, what the other person did or did not do should not shape your own integrity.

There are also those people who will beat themselves up over and over again for one mistake, unable to forgive themselves. Over time the inability to forgive yourself will degrade your sense of self-worth and self-esteem. It is virtually impossible to run a business if you are running low in these areas. Learning to forgive yourself is just as important as forgiving others. Take the lessons learned, use them, but break the emotional connection.

Being Trustworthy by Taking Inventory

What does it mean to be trustworthy? As I said in the beginning of the book, only 37 percent of employees trust their boss. That's a pretty low percentage. It implies they follow their CEO more out of necessity for a paying job than a connection to the work the company is doing. Where do you believe your staff would place you on that scale of perceived trust? Is it actually possible to make mistakes or poor decisions and still be trustworthy at the same time? My answer is yes.

You can no more completely remove imperfections than you can separate from your soul. However, that doesn't mean you have to accept your imperfections as they are. It is possible to strive for excellence in your daily life by not fearing those imperfections will sabotage your efforts along the way (Chopra, Ford, and Williamson 2010). It is much easier to drive around a pothole in the road when you can see it. Imperfections are no different and, once understood, you can work your way around them. By strengthening the best parts of yourself, you will no longer fear that someone may discover those imperfections that are holding you back.

I look at "imperfections" as the character traits that do not serve me well. To uncover those traits I use a process called "Fearless Moral Inventory" based on the process used in the AA Twelve-Step Process (Alcohol Anonymous 2002). What does it really mean to take a "fearless moral inventory of yourself" and why would you even want to look at those imperfections? Good question, because those traits may be holding you back or disengaging the people who work for you. The process is usually not as bad as it sounds. Quite often you will find some of your imperfections are really your strengths carried to extreme. I'll share more about that in a minute.

I created a simple table (shown as Table 4.1) to help me with my inventory process. The first column is my best assessment of thoughts, words, and deeds that have put me out of alignment with my core values. I have removed as much self-deception as possible and admitted that flaws exist. The second column is a specific example of where this occurred in my life and the last column is the steps I will take to prevent the action in the first column again. There is no right or wrong way to create a moral inventory or make your list. The most important thing is to do it on a regular basis.

Table 4.1 Fearless moral inventory

Truthful inventory	Specific example	Positive action
I have lied to others	I have lied to others to avoid being blamed for missing an important deadline for a project	Going forward I will ask for help rather than be embarrassed that I can't finish a project on my own without the help of others
I have pushed others beyond their limits without being asked to do so. I have become a "know it all"	I am passionate about helping others and have a real urge to jump in and "fix" a problem without asking permission first	I will offer help and get permission before saying anything. Without their permission, I will leave them to make their own decisions and learn the lessons from their choices
I am a perfectionist	I will not risk doing something if I don't believe it will turn out perfectly	I have learned to strive for excellence, allowing for mistakes and when something is "good enough" to get the job done
I am afraid to speak up when I disagree	I don't speak up for what I want out of fear of conflict	I am learning to let go of perceived conflict to decrease my fears
I am envious of what others have accomplished	I get upset when I should be further ahead in my career than others my age	I will be happy for what others have accomplished and more grateful for what I have
Add your own		

I find it very beneficial to date each list for continuity and watch my progress. Writing down each list is similar to journaling; it forces me to organize my thoughts creating clarity. Each time I write, I find it easier to become very specific as to the nature of my transgressions and become much clearer on the positive actions I need to take going forward and prevent slipping back in bad habits.

Getting back to strengths becoming weaknesses or imperfections. I'll use myself as an example. I tend to be a very decisive person. I size situations up quickly, make a decision, and then act on it. That works well sometimes, but there are other times when a better decision would have been made if I asked for other people's input. Being decisive is important but not when everyone else who has to act on those decisions feels left out of the process. Different leadership styles and decision-making processes are necessary to meet the ever-changing business situations. One size does not fit all (Goleman, Boyatzis, and McKee 2002).

Trust Partners

If you really want to push yourself there is another step you can take to push the boundaries on your inventory. This part requires working with a partner who is willing to challenge your self-assessment. I call this person a "trust partner," who will keep your confidences and not use your admitted personal shortcomings against you. You will both agree to challenge each other's assumptions, listen, and ask thoughtful questions about how you see yourself and how you believe others see you.

Your goal is not to agree, disagree, or compromise what you believe, but to help each other gain real clarity around self-perception. This is not something you can do with your staff and I wouldn't suggest using your spouse or significant others. That's a whole different book. The full details of this process can be found on my website and in the associate workbook *The Trust Factor Workbook.*

Thoughts for Reflection

- What pattern of behavior do you exhibit that allows others to feel that they can take advantage of you?
- What past hurts or wounds are you holding on to?
- Do you keep repeating the same stories of how others have hurt you?
- Are you willing to do the tough work of truly forgiving and releasing the toxicity you are carrying with you?
- Are you willing to look in the mirror and take a moral inventory of your own actions?
- Does the thought of "surrendering" frighten you or cause anxiety?
- There are so many questions raised by these topics to ask yourself. Take the time to think of the questions you wished I had asked. Read the chapter again if necessary before moving on.

CHAPTER 5

The Head and the Heart

If trust is the key to unlocking success, then it is important to understand the evolution of trust as it moves from its emotional drivers to intellectual thoughts and physical applications. To follow this process it's important to learn about the neuro connection between your heart and your head. It really opens the door for you as a leader to comprehend, empathize, and connect with the people in your organization. In fact, your ability to connect with all your stakeholders will predispose them to want to do business with you. People want to work for and do business with business owners they can trust.

Scientific research has long documented how your brain works in determining what is physically safe for you and what is not. The oldest part of your brain, the amygdala, has helped keep people alive for several millennium by recognizing danger quicker than the cognitive (thinking) part of your brain can comprehend it. Your amygdala is incredibly good at recognizing patterns and analyzing them in nanoseconds. This pattern recognition is the basis of your "fight or flight" survival mechanism. Your brain sees a pattern, analyzes it, and sends out chemical messengers to your entire body prepping you to fight or run away almost as fast as the speed of light.

In his incredible book *Thinking, Fast and Slow,* Nobel Laureate Daniel Kahneman goes into great detail on how lazy your brain really is and how your brain prefers to default to the "intuitive," fast-thinking primal brain rather than slower cognitive thinking. Why, because cognitive or deep thinking requiring problem solving or answering complicated questions tires you out, both mentally and physically. Ever noticed how tired and worn out you are after longer periods of focused mental effort? With an average weight of three pounds your brain is about two to three percent of your body weight. However, it consumes 20 percent of the calories you burn in a day. Your brain is a high powered, energy consuming engine.

Your brain self-regulates how much work it wants to do to avoid being tired. The research shows your brain defaults to find the most energy efficient way to get the job done. It is much more energy efficient to make assumptions and quick judgments based on what you believe rather than engage the energy consuming cognitive thinking in order to ask questions and reflect on answers.

Kahneman's research goes on to show how efficient your amygdala is at pattern recognition. As you see, hear, or even smell a pattern start to unfold, you quickly determine if the pattern is unleashing something safe or not safe. For example, you smell wood burning, the smell will quickly tell you if it is wood burning in a fireplace or something else is on fire that shouldn't be. The serpentine movement of a snake (even on a screen) is enough to set off a flight reaction.

Your senses pick up changes in energy in people and animals up to seven feet away, even when they are not in your direct line of sight. Have you ever sensed that someone was watching you, only to look up and find someone really looking at you? For me it usually happens in the car when stopped at a traffic light. Here is how that happens.

The Science of HeartMath

I learned about the HeartMath organization several years ago during my Conversational Intelligence® certification course. I found their work is fascinating to read because it connected a number of important pieces in the trust process. The HeartMath Institute has over 26 years of research into the neurological and chemical connection between your heart and your brain. Your heart actually sends more signals to your brain than your brain sends to your heart! Your heart has its own intrinsic, complex, and very organized nervous system which can adapt and reorganize itself by forming new neural connections quickly over an extended period of time, depending on what is happening in your life (McCraty Atkinson, Tomasino and Bradley 2009).

The neurological signals from your heart have a significant impact on your brain function. These signals influence your emotional processing and higher cognitive thinking such as attention, perception, memory, and problem solving. In other words, your heart and brain are connected by their own separate nervous system in a continuous loop of signals. If you think about it that makes sense as your body needs both these organs to live. Death occurs quickly when brain or heart function stops. This connection is incredibly strong and powerful. Because of this you need to be mindful of the impact one has on the other. Have you ever been so emotionally upset that you can't seem to think straight? You can't, your heart is overwhelming your brain with negative signals. Have you ever heard of someone overcoming sickness through mental willpower, the will to heal and live? You have and it is quite real, it's all in the head and heart connection.

So why do I believe you need to understand this head and heart connection? For several important reasons:

- You connect emotionally with others through your heart first. That emotion will either send a positive or negative signal to the brain before you even open your mouth.
- This is how your staff connects with you as a leader.
- It is the emotional connection that turns prospects into raving fans. It gives them that innate sense that you can help them achieve their goals by working with you.
- Lastly, in my opinion, it is in this connection that great leadership resides. The true connection of a clear mind and a passionate heart can accomplish virtually anything.

That's a lot to take in. There are millions of micro transactions taking place all day long inside of your body that you are not even aware of but have great impact on everything you do on a daily basis.

Mentally and emotionally, you process stimulus and information through your heart–brain connection all day long. Now I come back to the internal lens you filter everything through I talked about before. That lens is comprised of so many personal things you believe to be true. It includes but is not limited to:

- Your core values
- Accepted social norms and cultural upbringing
- Past experiences and traumatic events
- Education

- Religious beliefs and
- Your own self-limiting beliefs (self-sabotage)

The filters are too numerous to list. For now just know that they are there and impact what you think, say, and do.

Your Head–Heart connection and signal processing has often been called your intuition, or your "gut feeling." It takes place in your unconscious mind, no effort is required. It is no coincidence that the saying "gut feeling" comes out of the fact your stomach is located near your heart and that feelings hit you here first. How many times have you said to yourself, "I should have trusted my gut" or "I should have listened to my intuition," when a decision didn't go the way you planned? Developing your intuition is critical for making great decisions whenever "fast" thinking is required or slow the process down when more in depth thinking is required. However, when your lens is clouded it may throw your intuition off (Kahneman 2011, 12).

Your intuition can also lead you off course due to one other critical factor. A lack of clarity around your personal internal compass, your core values. Why, because I believe your core values have the strongest influence on how you perceive the world and those around you. Clarity around your core values can help hone your intuition to a razor's edge. Core values are your internal compass, they point you in a particular direction (North in a magnetic compass) before you even understand why. If your core values are not clear your internal compass will be pulled all over the place by outside pressure and influences. If your values are clear, your compass will point north without you thinking about it. Your core values define your magnetic field guiding you as you go (George 2007, 66).

Many leaders fail to consciously identify and define in writing, their top core values. You can feel them, but most cannot define the value when pressed to do so. This will tie in later on to help identify and define the values for your organization. This is not the same as the 37 pages Wells Fargo used to state their values. Didn't matter anyway, they obviously ignored all it.

Generally, your beliefs and core values are formed organically by default based on the influences I listed earlier. In Chapter 2, I explained that it would be impossible for you to guess what it would take to earn another person's trust. It is no different with core values, I don't know what your values are if you haven't identified and defined them. Your core values are what you stand for, they are your line in the sand that you will not cross. My first experience with core values came when I was a new Tenderfoot Boy Scout. The 12 Scout Laws first published in 1908 in *Scouting for Boys,* have been the core values recited by millions of scouts for over a hundred years.

A Scout is:

- Trustworthy
- Loyal
- Helpful
- Friendly
- Courteous
- Kind
- Obedient
- Cheerful
- Thrifty
- Brave
- Clean
- Reverent

It has been over 50 years since I first learned those values as a Tenderfoot Scout and I can still recite them today without hesitation. I didn't fully grasp the full weight of these values at the time, but I sure do appreciate them now! It is no accident that "Trustworthy" is at the top of the list.

Defining Core Values

Now it's your turn to identify and define your core values. This is critical work that will help you personally and professionally. As I said earlier, these are the values that will guide you through all the challenges you face. You define them and you live and work by them. Every time you don't abide by them you become out of alignment. There is a loss of integrity and one of the fastest ways for people to lose trust in you. Making mistakes makes you human and people will forgive. Violating your core values makes you untrustworthy and much tougher to gain that back (Table 5.1).

Table 5.1 Core values table

Accessibility	Faith	Merit	Security
Accomplishment	Fame	Mobility	Selfishness
Accountability	Family	Money	Self-Reliance
Accuracy	Fate		Seriousness
Achievement	Fitness	Non-Violence	Service
Adventure	Flair	Nurturing	Sexuality
Aspiration	Force		Simplicity
Attitude	Free will	Openness	Sincerity
Authenticity	Freedom	Opportunity	Skill
Authority	Fun	Optimism	Solidarity
Autonomy			Speed
	Generosity	Patriotism	Spirit-in-Life
Beauty	Giving/Charity	Peace	Stability
	Global View	Perfection	Standardization
Challenge	Goodness	Performance	Status
Change	Gratitude	Persistence	Strength
Chastity/Purity		Personal Growth	Style
Cleanliness	Hard Work	Philosophy	Success
Collaboration	Harmony	Pioneer Spirit	Support
Commitment	Heritage	Pleasure	Systemization
Communication	Heroism	Popularity	Satisfying Others
Community	Honesty	Positive Attitude	
Competence	Honor	Power	Teamwork
Competition	Hope	Practicality	Tolerance
Concern	Humor	Preservation	Tradition
Conformity		Prestige	Tranquility
Conviction	Improvement	Pride	Trust
Cooperation	Inclusiveness	Privacy	Truth
Courage	Influence	Prosperity/Wealth	
Creativity	Inner Peace	Punctuality	Utility
Customer	Innovation	Purity	
	Integrity		Variety

Decisiveness	Intuition	Quality	
Democracy	Involvement		Well-Being
Determination		Rationality	Wellness
Discipline	Joy	Recognition	Wisdom
Discovery	Justice	Regularity	
Diversity		Rehabilitation	
Duty	Knowledge	Reliability	
		Resourcefulness	
Education	Leadership	Respect	
Efficiency	Learning	Responsibility	
Empowerment	Leisure	Responsiveness	
Equality	Love-Care	Results-Oriented	
Excellence	Love-Concern	Risk-Taking	
Experience	Love-Romance	Rootedness	
Expression	Loyalty	Rule of Law	
Fairness	Meaning	Safety	

I was given this list of core values in a workshop years ago (author unknown). I use this list with the Core Values Exercise described below to help my clients identify their values. You can find many of these lists online if you don't like the one I have used. It's just a reference point to start you off.

As you read down the list some of these values will resonate with you, and some may not. That's okay. The purpose of the list is to help narrow down the choices and then pick those that mean the most to you. No two people will define any of the words on this list exactly the same way.

Core Values Exercise

Complete this exercise by doing the following:

- Get 10 index cards to write on.
- Write down one core value on each card, you can only have ten at any one time.
- The cards do not have to be in any particular order.

- Read each card out loud at the beginning of each day. You can add a new core value card at that time, but you must remove one at the same time.
- Read the cards out loud again at the end of the day. Same process, you can keep them all as is, or add and remove one.
- Do this exercise for an entire week. By the end of the week you should have arrived at your top 10 core values.
- When you think you have finished do the following:
  - Get a waste can or garbage pail.
  - Say the card out loud and then try to throw the card away.
  - If you reach a card you can throw away, you haven't finished. Start again.

It is perfectly normal to go through this process several times. Just keep doing this exercise over and over again until you get to the point where you cannot possibly throw any of those cards away. I've had clients call me and e-mail me with their frustration over making them do this exercise. I get it, this is not easy, I know because I've done it several times over the years. But I can tell you that I have not had one single complaint after the exercise was finished. The eventual benefits are limitless. Doing this exercise now will make it much easier when you decide the core values for your business. Some values may be the same, some may be different, but will know how to choose them.

If you thought that was challenging, now comes the tough part. Each core value must clearly be defined in two sentences or less and you cannot use the value itself in the definition. As you finish each definition write down why this value is important to you. You can write as much as you want here, include a story or any other relevant information. Use your journal or keep separate notes, whatever is easier for you. This second part of the Core Value exercise is designed to clarity on what the value means to you and why.

Be sure your core value definitions are clear, concise, easy to remember, and easy to articulate. I use this example of the definition of integrity—it is the simplest definition I've heard. "Say what you mean, mean what you say. Say what you will do and do what you say." There is no right or wrong here; it's your definition. But keep in mind, the more complicated or the vaguer your definition is, the harder it will be for you to keep to it.

Remember, these definitions are important for several reasons;

- Clarity about those qualities that are extremely important to you
- These are the values that best exemplify you as a person.
- Your ability to clearly articulate those values so others will know what you stand for and why. Don't assume others know intuitively what your values are.
- These values set your internal compass to help you navigate through business and life.
- They are the internal benchmarks you use to make decisions and take action that is in alignment with who you are.

Vaguely defined, unspoken core value are too easily violated by others and they will not know why. Do not place conditions on others to abide by your values; "If that person (loved me, cared for me, understood me, listened to me, respected me), they would not have said or done what they did." I can't tell you how often this one simple thing has disrupted working relationships and caused friction among team members. I'll talk more about that in the last section of this book.

I want to re-cap this chapter before moving on to the next section and the fundamentals of a corporate culture based on trust.

- The old part of your brain is amazing at recognizing patterns. It is your best tool for assessing each situation as it arises.
- The head and heart connection is bond between your passion and intellect. Too much of either one is overpowering. Your head guides the vision and your heart drives the action.
- Identify and define your core values to create a clear internal compass. This will guide your actions after a situation is assessed and the head-heart drivers kick in.

Do not underestimate the power of the head–heart connection. It is one of—if not the most—powerful tools you will have at our disposal to engage your staff and build a culture of trust. I finish here with this Japanese proverb—"Vision without action is a daydream, Action without vision is a nightmare."

Thoughts for Reflection

- What are your top core values?
- Are you clear why these values are so important to you?
- Do you expect others to intuitively understand your core values?
- Do you expect others to have the same values as you do?
- Do you use your values to judge others or unfairly expect them to live up to your standards?
- Do you take ownership when you have violated my own values and try and rationalize your decisions by blaming others?
- Do you ever feel like your head and your heart are at odds with each other?
- How often do you second guess your intuition?

PART II

Trust in Your Business— Foundational Building Blocks

CHAPTER 6

Setting the Foundation

I have always had a love of the water, oceans, rivers, streams, lakes, it doesn't matter. I find great peace when I am just looking at the ocean or being in or on the water. I've never questioned why, it just is. My love of the water led me to go to SUNY Maritime College in the Bronx, NY. The school is the longest running nautical school in the United States dating back to its founding in 1874 aboard the USS St. Mary's. The campus was moved ashore in the 1920s and located on the grounds of Fort Schuyler, a fort that was built in 1856 to guard the mouth of the Long Island Sound.

As a freshman cadet, I was required to memorize this saying, "The sea is selective, slow in recognition of effort and aptitude but quick in sinking the unfit." It's a quote from Felix Riesenberg, the school's superintendent from 1917 to 1919 and 1923 to 1924. I understood what the words said, but the full weight of their meaning didn't hit home until a few years later.

Instead of having summers off like most college students, the freshman, sophomore, and junior classes board the training ship and set out to sea for two and a half months. It was on the training ship I learned the tools of my trade, stood watch and learned how to be an officer. I crossed the Atlantic twice on our training ship and there is nothing like looking out and seeing nothing but the ocean and the horizon all around you. It is exciting and humbling at the same time.

Shipboard organization is run as a paramilitary organization; you have a captain, officers, and crew. It is highly structured for very important reasons, and trust in each other is essential for getting where you are going safely. There is a high degree of vulnerability between shipmates knowing help is not that close when you are in the middle of the ocean!

It's easy to be lulled into a false sense of security when the sea is calm and the sun is shining; however, that is not always the case. I vividly remember one night on my last cruise when my bunkmates and I felt the ship shudder and we were thrown from our bunks. Ships do not stop suddenly; it takes an awful lot of force to cause a ship to shudder and toss bodies out of beds. At first no one knew what had happened but I can tell you Felix's quote came quickly to mind and it was the first time I felt completely vulnerable while at sea. It ingrained in me the importance of being ever vigilant while on watch as there were sailors asleep below decks trusting me to keep them safe while they slept.

Fast forward another year and I am the Third Mate aboard the SS Samuel Mather on the Great Lakes. The other mates I worked with were more than twice my age and didn't appreciate a 22-year-old college-educated kid from Long Island, NY, being a ship's officer. They didn't trust anyone who didn't come up through the hausepipe (nautical term for working your way up from the bottom of the organizational ladder).

It took a little while for me to realize the lack of trust came from a fear of the unknown. It didn't look, sound, or act like anyone they had ever worked with. They couldn't comprehend how I had packed their 20 plus years of learning and experience into 4 years. I learned quickly that asking a lot of questions and being open to them "teaching" me what they knew eased their distrust. I was never fully accepted—the gap created by difference in age, knowledge, and perceived experience was too big—but it did make working together much easier.

I share these stories to show how my adult concepts of trust were shaped and to highlight why trust does not appear to be as important in working together as it should. You live in tight quarters on board a ship and for better or worse, you get to know your shipmates pretty well. In the corporate workplace most employees are insulated from each other by the work they do and have lives outside of work. Their life begins again as soon as the work day is done and trust is not necessarily essential for staying alive. It is easy to assume that employees trust each other because in many businesses your staff member's daily lives don't depend on high levels of trust inside your organization. The level of trust within the status quo is good enough.

However, good is the anathema to great when another competitor or alternative comes along to disrupt what you are doing (Collins 2001). Think how disruptive Uber and Airbnb were to two very traditional industries. A livery service that owns no vehicles and a hotel company with no owned hotels. Hotels have since lobbied hard to have Airbnb play by their rules and NYC Taxi medallions once worth millions are worth a fraction of that now. Airbnb was so disruptively successful it went from a startup in 2008 to $1.6 billion in revenue by 2017.

After coaching for a few years I knew the knowledge and experience of running a business was not enough to help CEOs and their businesses the way I wanted to. I decided to become a student of business to enhance my coaching. Fortunately, Vistage International, the organization I was coaching for at the time, offered to pay half of MBA so I could better serve our mutual clients. I jumped at the chance and after two straight years of studying nights and weekends (I was still working full time) I finished my MBA in Organizational Development.

Why do it? Why go back to graduate school 20 years after college? I knew my skill set was good enough to work with clients but not great; my clients deserve great. All the professors, authors I met were incredible. They expanded my understanding of business, and organizational development in particular, in a way that I could not experience in a single lifetime. Thanks to video conferencing, I was able to work with students from around the globe and see live some of the industry giants who literally wrote the textbooks we were using. I'll not forget sitting and listening to Michael E. Porter discuss his book *Competitive Advantage, Creating and Sustain Superior Performance*. I'll admit to being a business geek, but it was fascinating to listen how the author put all of his thoughts and research into context for students to study and implement.

Over the past decades I have read hundreds of books on leadership, leading change, organizational structure, and corporate culture. I enjoy reading others' perception of how people and process should go together to create value. Obviously every author has their opinion on what works, what doesn't, or how to get the most out of your employees. The concept and importance of trust in the workplace is often referenced, but not given the weight it deserves. Trust in the workplace is similar to the friction-based connection between two or more Lego© parts. No glue or other fastener is required and all the Lego© pieces use this patented connection to fit together. However, it is the emotional bond between people that makes us stick instead of friction.

There are a number of prominent businesses that have used trust as the underlying foundation for working together. One of my favorite examples of this is Gore, Inc. I first studied Gore during my MBA course and have been a fan ever since. Here is a brief summary of an interview with the CEO Terri L. Kelly about Gore's corporate structure. This is part of what she said:

> "Gore is a $2.4bn, hi-tech materials company that most people know best for the Gore-Tex fabric that waterproofs their anoraks and walking boots—no one can tell any of the company's 8,500 associates what to do. Although there is a structure (divisions, business units and so on) there is no organization chart, no hierarchy and therefore no bosses. I am (Kelly) one of the few with a title."
>
> At Gore—As she acknowledges, that makes her job rather different from that of most CEOs. Bill Gore, who set up the company with his wife Vieve (short for Genevieve) in the family garage in 1958, wanted to build a firm that was truly innovative. So there were no rule books or bureaucracy. He strongly believed that people come to work to do well and do the right thing. Trust, peer pressure and the desire to invent great products—market-leading guitar strings, dental floss, fuel cells, cardiovascular and surgical applications and all kinds of specialized fabrics—would be the glue holding the company together, rather than the official procedures other companies rely on. (Caulkin 2008)

Bill Gore was certainly ahead of his time and the company continues to innovate and thrive today using the same principles it was founded on over 60 years ago. It remains one of those rare companies that has not succumbed to the daily results and bottom-line pressure of Wall Street investing. I truly believe going forward, this type of culture will provide the best competitive edge for any business in any industry. The long-term financial results are there and the best future employees will be attracted to it.

There has been a lot of innovation and shifts in culture away from the more traditional workplaces. Google has office complexes or campuses complete with slides from floor to floor in some locations. Other companies have changed dress codes, created sleep pods, happy hour carts on

Friday afternoon, lounges, and many other creative ways for employees to relax and be more comfortable at work. Nothing, however, will replace the feelings of being safe, respected, and appreciated. Trust comes first; everything after that is a plus.

The next several chapters will dig into what destroys trust in your organization and what you can do to build it. Then I will take you through some of the basics that apply to, sole practitioners, partnerships, corporations (for profit and not-for-profit), and family businesses to see how trust applies to all of them. The fundamentals are the same because every structure still depends on employees.

Thoughts for Reflection

- Can you envision how the connectivity of trust in your organization can be a real competitive edge on many levels?
- Does it make sense why your current culture will either attract or repel certain types of people?
- Are the core values for your business clearly defined?
- Are you clear about the core values you want in your future employees?
- Will your current culture attract the employees that fit with those values?
- Do you and your employees "walk you talk"?

CHAPTER 7

Trust Killers and Builders

If you are like most CEOs you have worked hard to be an expert in your industry and understand the operational elements (Operations, Sales, IT, Finance, HR, etc.) required to get the work done. You can hire people to do this work or you can outsource the work to other professionals. There is one thing you cannot outsource for others to manage, your culture.

The culture of your business starts at the top with you and the core values that define how you will conduct business. Building and sustaining a culture based on trust requires different skillsets that are not traditionally taught. These are the people-orientated skills that will enable you to engage your employees in a very different level. Conversational, relational, mindfulness, and emotional intelligence become essential skills for employee engagement. These skills are usually learned experientially making them difficult to teach in the traditional way.

You may be very strong at some of these skills already, that's great and you can then focus more time on other skills that may not be as strong. You will tend to gravitate to your stronger skills, those you feel most comfortable with. The others may be more challenging because typically you have avoided them because they push you out of your comfort zone.

Building trust in your organization starts with an awareness of these skills, clarity about core values and the ability to express yourself. By this I mean you can clearly articulate what you are thinking and feeling at any time. I cannot stress enough how important the words you use are to creating the success you want.

Expressing yourself however, doesn't mean you just say what you want, when you want, to others or yourself without thinking first! Take time to reflect and be mindful of the words you use when speaking. It takes no skill at all to crush yourself or others in an instant with a careless word or tone of voice. Listen to yourself as you speak. Do the words and the tone coming out of your mouth reflect who you really want to be? In your head who was really speaking? I'll talk more in a minute about your parental self, your teen self or your angry child self, showing up instead of the mature adult. Listening and reflecting on what you say is a great way to develop more self-awareness and leads to making better choices in how you communicate with others. Practice makes you better at any skill and you can learn how to speak to be understood.

Conversational skills usually take the form of a public-speaking course taught in high school, graduate school, or organizations like Toastmaster International. This is not the conversational skills I am discussing. I'll go into greater detail when I discuss Conversational Intelligence©. The point I want to make here is that effective conversational skills are rarely taught. Even worse is that fact combined with the conversational role modeling of highly paid "real" people on "reality shows" where the verbal character assassination skills are highly valued. This is how we are teaching generations of employees how to talk to each other? Drama, emotional tirades, and verbal abuse are not the way to successfully talk out tough situations when they come up. The best way is to have a safe enough space that encourages open, honest, and trusting communication.

Now I'll discuss the patterns of behavior, action, and conversation that either kill trust or encourage it. Some of these will seem quite obvious when reading about them and easier to recognize in others than yourself. Remember, as the champion of trust you must be able to recognize these behaviors in yourself before bringing them up to others.

Trust Killer #1—Rushing to Judgment

Rushing to judgment is a devastating habit and one that is done for a variety of reasons. For the purpose of this book, I will define judgment as your opinion stated as fact. You are entitled to your own opinions and beliefs, everyone has that right. However, when you state your opinions as facts, you do not leave room for anyone else's opinion. In *Thinking, Fast and Slow*, Daniel Kahneman uses decades of scientific study to explain how and why judgment happens in your brains. For my purposes there are two primary reasons for judgment:

1. Judgment is quick and easy. The other person is right or wrong based on the way you feel things should be. Your brain is lazy and likes quick and easy thinking. Judgment avoids deeper more cognitive thought.

2. Your judgment always allows you to be right all the time. It does not matter what the other person is doing, you just know your assessment of them being right or wrong is always correct. Believing you are right releases the "feel good" chemical oxytocin in your system. Being right literally makes you feel good and we all like feeling good. That creates a desire to get more of that feeling and "being right" makes that happen. Judgment becomes a habit to keep feeling good.

Judgment creates thinking that is centered on what is good or bad, appropriate or inappropriate—right down to how others look, talk, dress, cars they drive, where they live, or how much money they make. When judgment occurs conversations either shut down or become a meaningless debate, with each person defending their own set of "facts" because no one wants to be wrong. In these types of debates nothing is gained and nothing is learned. These arguments generally escalate, because now you want to not only prove you are right, but why the other person is so wrong. Have you ever been in a meeting that has escalated into a hopeless deadlock of defended positions? Utter waste of time in my estimation and it breaks down the bonds between us very quickly. It is very difficult to trust someone who is constantly judging others. Judgment kills trust.

Trust Killer #2—Making Assumptions

Making assumptions is another widespread habit that kills trust for the same two reasons I outline in judgment, assumptions are quick and easy and you're always right. Plus, one important addition, making assumptions is far less risky than to ask a question. Asking questions can open you up to examination by others, appearing foolish or stupid because you didn't already know the answer or embarrassed because you get publicly rebuffed just for asking. Making assumptions also avoids having to ask questions that you may not want to hear the answer. Fear of embarrassment and rejection are two huge motivators to make assumptions rather than seek answers.

Assumptions go hand in hand with judgment. In any given situation you can make an assumption, judge it, and be satisfied with your conclusions without anyone else knowing how you got there (Senge 2000). Now once your assumption has been made, any challenge to it must be met with a vigorous defense. Have you ever engaged in a conversation with someone who knows their previous assumption was incorrect but goes to extraordinary lengths to explain why they were correct in that assumption? That person loses all integrity, severely damaging any trust between you. Imagine for one second, instead of defending their position, the other person said "Actually, that was a poor assumption on my part and I was incorrect," or something along those lines. Would you be more inclined to engage in further conversations knowing this person was willing to admit to a mistake?

If I could eliminate one thing from your organization's decision making process it would be making assumptions. I'll lay the groundwork here and then complete it in Part III of the book. To break making assumptions you have to put the quick thinking (Kahneman 2011) process into slow motion. Here's what I mean. The process always starts with sensory input. That input can be almost anything, sight, sound, smell and then:

- Using the pattern analysis of past experiences your amygdala (survival part of the brain) quickly decides if the input is positive or negative.
- Chemicals are released flipping your cells up or down priming your thoughts and feels to be positive or negative.
- You assume that "I've seen, felt, done this before" and are already primed, positive or negative, this will be the same.
- Any further input is now filtered through a negatively or positively charged lens.
- This causes a biased interpretation of the input creating further assumptions.
- Conclusions are drawn based on your judgment and action taken.

Hence the term "jumping to conclusions" is really a series of chemical reactions, quick thinking assumptions and judgments leading to a conclusion in record time. To stop making assumptions the cycle has to be broken. In a business setting this happens several ways:

- Challenge the pattern recognition, what was friend or foe in the past may not be the same now.
- You will have a chemical reaction to the stimulus, that's ok. Stop and discern how the input could be different now.
- Don't assume you know what is going on or that you know what is coming next.
- Making the environment safe to ask good questions without fear of embarrassment or retaliation. Asking questions also slows this process down quickly to allow time for the chemical reaction to die down.
- Seek to understand all aspects of the stimulus before coming to any conclusions.

Breaking the habit of making assumptions is critical to maintain the integrity of trust between everyone in your organization. As the CEO you are the role model for not jumping to conclusions and instead asking great questions. Telling others not to make assumptions while you still do never works. It is almost always implied "if the CEO behaves or acts in a certain way then it is ok for us do it as well."

Trust Killer #3—Emotional Hijacking

The concept of "emotional hijacking" has been around for decades. In his 1995 book *Emotional Intelligence*, Dr. Daniel Goleman describes the process whereby the "thinking" part of your brain can literally be shut down, or "hijacked," by your emotional response to a person, event or other stimulus. I mentioned earlier that your brain can get overloaded with emotional input to the point where you have trouble staying focused. I have personally seen people faint, cry inconsolably for hours, go completely silent, or just stare blankly ahead upon hearing bad news or witnessing a traumatic event.

The rush of adrenaline mixed with cortisol can cause your brain to shut down all non-life-threatening functions in an instant. Have you ever been so angry that, later on, you don't even remember what you said? As Daniel Goleman puts it, "you lose it." You take out your emotions on whoever is handy—a spouse, child, friend, co-worker, employee or sometimes even a complete stranger. It takes only an instant for you to "lose it," but its impact can last a lifetime. While you may not remember what you said, the person on the other end of your tirade will. And, once something is said, it is almost impossible to take back.

You are human just like the rest of us and it is normal from time to time to "lose it," I know I have and it wasn't pretty. It takes a lot to get me angry, but you don't want to be around me when I am.

In Super Brain creator Jim Kwik's masterclass *How to Develop a Super Memory*, I learned a simple method to de-escalate your brains from emotional triggers. To help remember his process he uses the acronym ABRA (think abracadabra!).

- The first step is to <u>A</u>cknowledge and become aware of when you are being triggered.
- The second step is to <u>B</u>reathe. Deep breathing can take many forms and oxygen flow is crucial to helping us relax and de-stress.
- The third step is to <u>R</u>elease, let go of the feeling and allow it to pass. Don't try to suppress it—just let it pass out of you as you breathe out.
- The last step is to Align. Set your mind on a positive outcome and extend your compassion to the other person, you don't know what is going on inside them.

I've used this process and for me, it works!

The good news is you can learn to read your own personal warning signs and break this hijacking or at least limit its duration. Who wants to be around someone who blows up all the time? You don't trust them to be in control and become afraid they will take out their emotions on you. Breaking undesirable behavioral patterns such as emotional hijacking is a huge piece to emotional freedom and I will discuss that later on in this chapter.

There is also a big difference between controlling and mastering of emotions. The idea of control suggests you can stop or prevent your emotions from happening. This has a disastrous effect on your ability to relate to others. Remember that you connect and build trust first emotionally and then intellectually. It is also unhealthy to try and control your emotions. Internalizing emotions wreaks havoc on your internal organs, immune and nervous systems. Quite frankly, every part of the body is affected. Trying to control emotions can also lead to self-medication through alcohol use or drugs. Once the self-medication wears off, your reality creeps back in and the desire to shut it out starts the vicious cycle all over again.

Negative or destructive emotions are as much a part of you as positive ones. Learning to understand and recognize the "triggers" that push your buttons is the first step to emotional mastery. Buddhism has a practice called "observing in equanimity" (grace under fire). It requires observing events or experiences in a nonjudgmental state of mind with no emotional attachment. The idea is that all events are neutral until you assign a meaning.

It sounds plausible; however, I am not sure I want to go through life not assigning meaning or emotions to events. I can't experience true joy and happiness without having experienced deep sorrow. At the same time, I don't want to be ruled or hijacked by my emotions. Mastery is the ability to allow my emotions to come up and then be effectively channeled into positive actions. The first and most basic step is to not allow yourself to get too tired, too hungry, or not give your brain and body a chance to rest. Any one of these states can make you susceptible to emotional hijacking, and experiencing all three at once is an emotional ticking time bomb.

The next step is to recognize your personal triggers. How do you feel? For me, it can be as simple as losing my patience, getting quickly aggravated or short-tempered. During my divorce just seeing my ex-wife's name come up on caller ID would put my stomach in a knot. Feelings like this are not my normal response to a phone call, so I know I've been triggered. I used to react to these feelings not knowing I had a choice. Now, as they come up, I am quick to recognize that I have been triggered. I breathe, allow the feeling to pass and make a choice as to how I am going to respond. Once the emotion passes, my higher thinking can kick in, allowing me to think rather than react.

Trust Killer #4—The Parent, Adult, and Child

Research on cognitive behavior describes three different basic mindsets that you operate from at any given time: the critical parent, the level-headed adult, and the rebellious child (Berne 1973). The critical parent is where you know better and you are going to teach or educate the other person on why you are right and they are wrong. You are operating from a mentally superior attitude. The rebellious child comes from the grown person on the receiving end of the interaction with the critical parent. It tends to be a more immature emotional reaction prompting the critical parent to get even more critical. Sarcasm, scolding, ridicule, temper flare-ups, and jokes at the other's expense typify the interactions between two or more people acting this way.

The adult mindset is different, all the people involved in the inter-action are to be considered and respected as adults. Conversations and questions are inquiring rather than an inquisition. You can be emotion-ally engaged but not emotionally hijacked. Being an adult requires a sense of awareness so as not be triggered into a critical parent or rebellious child state of mind. Have you ever felt that a peer was talking to you like a par-ent? Did you feel your emotions rise because they were not treating you as an adult? Have you caught yourself speaking to another adult in your parental voice without realizing it?

None of us enjoys being treated in any way other than as an adult. It is demeaning and kills trust quickly. Adults should always be treated to and spoken to as an adult whether they are acting like an adult or not. If you catch yourself being anything other than adult, stop, pause, breathe, and start over again. You will feel much better for it and so will the other person.

Other Trust Killers in the Corporate World

The trust killers mentioned above can be found everywhere. Here are some of the more visible trust killers found in the corporate world. They destroy trust at any level of an organization:

- Not being transparent as a leader
- Taking credit for other people's work

- Not keeping confidences
- Micromanaging
- Not keeping commitments
- Not leading by example
- Status over Results
- Popularity over Accountability
- Certainty over Clarity
- Harmony over Conflict
- Invulnerability over Trust

There is some overlap for sure, but these trust killers show up in every organization to sabotage your working relationships, effectiveness, and results (Lencioni 1998). These trust killers are by no means an exhaustive list of all the things that kill trust in an organization, but they are a good place to start.

Now it is time to move on to the positive things you can do right away to build trust in your organization. It is far more empowering and exciting to focus on positive action. Let these positive actions squeeze out negative behavior because there will be no room for it.

Trust Builder #1—Being Vulnerable

I intentionally put this one first! Vulnerability opens the door for trust to start. I've already discussed why putting on armor (Brown 2014) limits your ability to emotionally connect with your staff and limits your abilities as a leader. Vulnerability is about being open to other people's thoughts and ideas, emotionally connected with your-self and others and willing to admit you make mistakes. You can be a strong, decisive, engaging leader and humble at the same time, it is not counter-intuitive.

Being vulnerable does not require exposing inner fears, or a high level of personal disclosure. What you are willing to disclose or not depends on who you are engaged with and the situation. It is possible to be vulnerable and reasonably safe at the same time. I know conformity to social norms place huge pressure on the need to protect your ego, how you perceive that others see you. Vulnerability in the past has been considered a real weakness in men while socially accepted in woman because they are weak. Just the opposite is true. Real men are supposed to tough it out, do it alone, don't show emotion or cry, I don't talk about my feelings and so on. That sounds more like a rock than a person. Women on the other hand, have proven time and time again they can be vulnerable and strong at the same time. Vulnerability like any other behavior when taken to the extreme becomes a weakness. Being vulnerable does not mean emotionally falling apart or exposing intimate details of your life.

I also believe being vulnerable requires you not to avoid dealing with your or others emotions. Trust requires you to lean in when someone else is hurt, crying, upset, frustrated or shows other painful emotion. How comfortable you are with other people's emotions is in direct proportion to how comfortable you are with your own. That's a whole different book. For now, just reframe you concepts around being vulnerable, you can be strong and safe at the same time.

Trust Builder #2—Empathy

I said earlier vulnerability opens the door for trust to begin, empathy then keeps the door open. I didn't understand empathy at all. It was a concept that eluded me and quite frankly bothered me when others seemed to get so emotionally wrapped up in what I considered to be other people's drama. What I didn't understand is that during my first marriage I armored up from head to toe to make sure the negative emotions didn't get in. I didn't realize it was still on after my divorce. That all changed when I married my second wife Lisa. My wife is a true empath, she physically feels other people's emotions. Human beings all have mirror neurons that allow us to emotionally connect with each other. Dogs have very similar mirror neurons which is why they can sense what is going on you and you can feel a bond with them.

Empaths like my wife have a heightened sense of connection, far greater than mine. She is keenly aware to the emotions and energy of the people around her and her physical surroundings. Lisa can quickly read other peoples energy and determine what mood they are in. At the time all I could see (not feel) the outward signs of what was going on for someone. As a result, within minutes of us going to a public place complete strangers would be telling my wife their life story. They can feel her empathy and that makes them feel safe enough to share.

Over time I realized how much I was missing by not being more open to my feelings. I was safe, it was ok, and Lisa would never manipulate my feelings to hurt me or get what she wants. I also wanted to connect with my 12-year-old step-daughter Samantha or Samm as she prefers to be called. Samm has a wisdom and love far more mature than people twice her age. I didn't have children in my first marriage and now I had the family I always wanted. How could I not open my heart to love these two women who loved me?

Feelings are the gateway to empathy as it became my conscious choice to be vulnerable enough to extend my compassion and be open to the feelings someone else is having. My wife taught me I can do this without worrying about being hurt because I will be hurt. You cannot feel without being hurt at different times. That makes us human.

I came across an incredibly powerful poem years ago in one of my coaching workshops. It is called *The Invitation* by Oriah Mountain Dreamer and for me personally speaks directly to my heart about empathy. Here is one small section:

> It doesn't interest me who you know or how you came to be here.
> I want to know if you will stand in the centre of the fire with me
> and not shrink back.

Understanding and being empathetic was a huge shift for me. All of my prior leadership training focused more on self-control and not showing a lot of emotion. But my staff couldn't connect with me on an emotional level because I wouldn't let them in. Why should I? As long as everyone showed up and did their work on time all was good. The trouble with that was, without an emotional connection to me they didn't feel connected to their work. It was never going to be more than a job to them and I was never going to get their best effort.

I changed my focus from what was important to who was important in my life. Empathy requires you to actually care about other people, you cannot fake it, don't even try. False empathy comes across as insincerity and is one of the fastest ways to have others want to disconnect from you.

If you struggle with empathy, admit it. Tell the other person you do not know how they are feeling, I do. When I am not sure I'll ask "Help me understand what you are feeling right now" or "Can you share with me what brought these feelings on?" Making an assumption I understood their feelings devalued the relationship. Employees really appreciate when you take the time and make the effort to understand what they are feeling.

Trust Builder #3—Asking Questions

Asking questions and actually listening to the answers is a key ingredient for building trust. Asking "yes" or "no" questions doesn't invite informative answers and rarely gives you the information you need to ask follow-up questions. Others will judge you based on the type of questions you ask. The more thoughtful the question, the more likely the other person will start to connect with you on a deeper level. My grandfather used to say, "A smart man has all the answers; a wise man knows how to ask great questions."

Asking questions however, does not mean giving advice in the form of a question. For example, "Have you ever thought about splitting the sales team into geographic regions?" is not a question. It is the suggestion of splitting the sales team into geographic regions. You believe you know the answer, but your suggestion appears safer and less confrontational then just telling them you have the answer. That type of suggestion forces the other person to a) accept the suggestion effectively ending the conversation with no further discovery or b) reject the suggestion and defend their primary position to avoid possible embarrassment because they should have thought of that idea.

Ask open ended-questions, or questions for which you have no answer (Glaser 2014). The open ended question would be "What would be the best way to organize the sales teams to make them more effective?" You can't answer that yes or no, it requires possible research, thought, and discussion before arriving at an answer. This type of question opens up a conversation and gives everyone the opportunity to explore options together rather than close them off. Seems simple enough, right? Yet so many conversations are shut down simply because no one is willing to risk asking a question for which they have no answer!

Practice making an effort to ask questions that avoid suggestions or judgments, then think of follow-up questions. The follow up can be as simple as "Can you say more?" or "What makes you think that?" up to very specific questions based on the answers given.

You can practice asking questions with your family, friends, and practically anyone you meet. See how it makes you feel opening up to people and making them smile by asking questions and really caring about their answers. Above all, if you are going to ask questions, please let the person respond before speaking again and genuinely be interested in their answers! You can quickly tell when someone is not interested in what you are saying and others can too when you are not listening to them.

Trust Builder #4 – Listening

Listening is the flip side of asking great questions. It allows you to ask another great follow up question. This quote has stuck with me since I heard it years ago. "Being listened to feels so much like being loved, you are hard pressed to tell the difference" (Augsburger 1982). How does it make you feel when you believe someone is listening carefully to what you have to say or asks you a question and is honestly interested in your response? Can you feel a connection?

There has been a lot written about listening—the 80/20 rule, listen 80 percent and speak 20 percent. You have two ears and one mouth for a reason. So you are listening by repeating back what you have heard and so on. It all sounds like sound advice, but that's all about hearing, listening is different and takes more effort. I'll give you an example and then give you the steps I use to develop listening skills.

I was working with one individual who was hired by a family business to act as interim CEO of a family business until the next generation was ready to take over. Chris was a smart guy and had run several other businesses as an interim CEO as well. The family started getting feedback from long-term employees that Chris wasn't listening to them and they were struggling to communicate. They asked if I could work with Chris on his communication skills with employees. Chris and I sat down to talk and I will not forget what he had to say about listening;

Russ, I get the sense that the employees equate my listening to them with actually acting on the suggestions they make. I hear them, I'm listening, it's just that I usually disagree with them, thank them for their input and move on to the next thing I have to do. I'm not understanding their problem.

Wait, what? It took me a second to digest what Chris said. He heard them so in his mind he was listening but didn't think any further action was required other than giving a few minutes of his time. Some may think that is rude, he just felt it was expedient. I knew it was unproductive, causing friction and going to create unnecessary problems in the future. Chris had been a CEO for so long he had lost touch with what it was like to work for a boss. As long as everyone listened and did what he had to say everything was ok, but it wasn't. Here is the context and the guidelines I gave him for listening:

Great leaders connect with their staff, to do this you must not just hear them but listen by doing the following:

- Turn off distractions when possible. That includes TVs, computer screens, radios, or other noises. The human voice can convey an incredible range of feeling and emotion. Don't miss what is being conveyed because you can't hear the other person.
- Be present. Please do not look up, down, at other people, or at your phone, tablet, computer or other device. You don't have to stare into their eyes the whole time—that gets weird. But make eye contact periodically and stay focused on their face.
- Do not speak or interrupt until the other person has finished speaking.
- Work hard at not formulating an answer, or your next question while they are talking. You will miss part of what they are saying because you are too busy listening to your internal conversation rather than the external one.
- Learn to ask follow up questions or for clarification of what you heard.

- Be curious and interested. You will be amazed at what other people have to share!

When asking questions the same rules apply plus:

- Do not speak or ask another question until the question has been answered.
- A slower response or silence is ok because the other person may be working through their thoughts to formulate an answer.
- Waiting for a response may feel a little awkward, but learn to wait, you will get a much better answer by not rushing the other person.

Listening is one of the most effective and powerful tools you can use as a leader, use it wisely.

Trust Builder #5—Discernment

The term discernment is not used all that often, the word judgment is far more recognized and used in communication. They are not the same, there is a big difference between the two. I explain discernment as your perception of people and events without labeling them right or wrong, good or bad, and so on. Observe and assess without putting a spin on it to gain a better understanding of what you are hearing or seeing. Judgment as I said earlier eliminates the need for further inquiry, you assume you already know what is going on.

Discernment almost always leads to questions, further inquiry, discovery, and a desire to learn more before arriving at any conclusion. Start from the point of reference that you know nothing and need to learn more. This thinking opens your mind to take in more information rather than discarding it as irrelevant. Discernment also hones your skill of perception (less filtering) by the heart–brain connection of emotion and intellect. It requires listening to understand, caring and asking an open-ended question for which you have no answer. Enhanced perception in turn fine-tunes your intuition (pattern recognition feedback loop) and become more adept at making better decisions.

Another real benefit and true trust builder is that other people will feel safer and connected when you are seeking to understand them rather than judging them. No one I know likes the feeling of being judged.

Finally, discernment helps break the habit of making assumptions and hasty judgments. If you catch yourself doing either of those things, stop and ask yourself the following questions:

1. Why have I chosen this course of action? Are there other actions I should have considered?
2. What belief do I have that lead to this action? Was that belief well-founded?
3. What am I assuming, and why? Are my assumptions valid?
4. Was there data I could have used or discovered to avoid making assumptions?
5. What are the real facts that I should be using? Are there other facts I should consider?
6. How did I come to that conclusion? Is the conclusion sound?

There are a lot of other questions you can ask yourself to debrief and reflect on the choices you make and the actions you take. Discernment creates a lot of positive dividends besides trust and is one action that can help constantly polish your lens.

Trust Builder #6—Integrity

Your personal integrity is non-negotiable when building and sustaining trust in your organization. Say what you mean, mean what you say. Honor your commitments and follow through with them. There are no careless words for leaders, be careful what you say and the commitments you make, you will be expected to honor them. There are few things in life that will destroy trust faster, than believing you have an agreement with someone to do something, in an agreed-upon manner, and then they (a) don't fulfill their obligation or worse, (b) do something completely the opposite of what was agreed to.

Don't make commitments lightly; the others in your life will not. Quoting my wise grandfather yet again, "The only thing no one can ever take away from you is your word. It defines who you are." Your word is your commitment, give it thoughtfully and carefully.

Lastly, as part of your integrity create personal standards. Standards, unlike rules (which are given to you by others), are your internal drivers that become the outward expression of the core values you determined earlier. These standards are how you conduct yourself—whether anyone is watching or not.

My choice as a standard for personal integrity are *The Four Agreements* by Don Miguel Ruiz. His agreements or terms for integrity are simple and concise:

- Be impeccable with your word
- Do not take things personally
- Don't make assumptions
- Always do your best

Words have the power to both create and to destroy. Impeccable means being careful and deliberate with each word you use. Not taking things personally or making assumptions (already discussed) is far harder to do than it sounds. We are all trained to take things personally; it may be hard to take but the world does not revolve around your personal life. Doing your best means accepting that your best will change on a daily basis. There will be some days when you feel you can conquer the world, and others when you're the bug on the windshield. The most important thing is to keep a positive mindset and do your best at any given moment (Ruiz 2000).

Create your own, here is one example I have given to others that they found helpful. In his autobiography, Benjamin Franklin created a list of his personal standards. Here are a few of his "thirteen standards for living" (Franklin 2016, pp. 88–89) and what I perceive is the core value behind it:

- Less Talk, More Action—"Well done is better than well said." (Core Value – Accomplishment)
- Get Moving—"Mankind is divided into three classes: immovable, movable, and those that move." (Core Value – Risk-Taking)

- Know Yourself—"There are three things extremely hard: steel, a diamond, and knowing one's self." (Core Value – Personal Growth)
- Don't Give Up—"Energy and persistence conquer all things." (Core Value – Persistence)

No one can tell you or force you to do these things. Personal integrity and living by your standards will clearly set you apart from others. Holding your standards allows others to feel safe in putting their trust in you.

I'll share a quick story about integrity and being trustworthy. A few years into my insurance career I had a meeting with a prospective client that would significantly alter my concepts of trust and selling forever. I was referred by my accountant to a kosher caterer located in a local temple. They were having trouble with their current insurance company and asked if he knew anyone who could help.

I met with the caterer and came up with a proposal very much to his liking. However, before we could do business I had to meet with the Rabbi and get his approval. I didn't think much about the meeting until I met with the Rabbi in his office. He welcomed me in with a kind smile and asked me to sit down in front of his desk. After I introduced myself his face became solemn and he leaned across his desk, looked me in the eye and said "Why should I do business with you, tell me why I should trust you?" and then sat back in his chair. I had to pause for a minute, no one had ever asked me those questions before. My mind was racing, had I done something wrong, had I offended him? Normally I am not at a loss for words but I sure was this time.

The Rabbi smiled as he could see I was struggling and put me at ease. He then shared one of the best lessons on "selling" that I still remember many decades later. The Rabbi said "I see you are struggling, so do you know why I asked you those questions? It is because insurance is a promise to do something when and if something bad happens. I need to know now that I can trust you, so that I do not have to worry about a problem in the future. This insurance company is only as good as you are." I thanked him for both the opportunity, his insight and ultimately their business. I've never forgotten that meeting and his words launching me on the search for more information on selling an intangible.

A few years later I had my friend Mitch Tobol's marketing firm do some research as to why my clients did business with me. Was it due to professional service, competitive rates, responsive to their requests, or some other aspect of service or insurance offerings? Several weeks later Mitch came back to me and said "Russ, we got the same answer over and over again. Your clients do business with you for one very important reason, it's not the insurance companies you have or the rates you charge. It's your personal integrity and the relationship they feel they have with you, they know you and they trust you." I asked him if he had any additional information as to why they felt this way. Mitch just smiled and said "It's the same reason why you and I are friends, I know you genuinely care about me as a person."

I suppose I should have known that I attracted clients who valued relationships as much as I did, especially when selling an intangible item. My clients wanted someone they could know and trust to do the right thing for them so they didn't have to worry who would help them when a claim occurred. Prospects who didn't value a relationship and shopped primarily for price would never be my client as it is impossible for me to always have the lowest price. The most important thing to remember is this, personal integrity is everything. For employees, clients, prospects, and all your stakeholders to trust you, you must remain trustworthy.

Trust Builder #7—Breaking Old Patterns

I wrote earlier that your brain, specifically the amygdala, is extremely good at recognizing patterns. Those patterns can be in your words, your tone of voice, your actions, and right down to the clothes you are wearing that day. Your staff hears a certain tone in your voice and they think "here we go again, here comes that speech again about not enough sales." Or, you show up in clothes other than what you normally wear and they want to know what's going on? In the absence of information, people make stuff up.

The idea here is to create more patterns of behavior around the trust builders and diminish the patterns around the trust killers. We want the staff to be triggered in a positive way rather than a negative one. There are literally millions of articles written on how to break behaviors that don't serve you well. In their book *Imagine All Better* by (Crowley and Kublis 2012), Dr. Crowley succinctly describes why you just can't tell yourself to stop certain behaviors. He has allowed me to share a small part of his work because I felt my summary would not do it justice:

How to Easily Break Repeating Behavior Patterns;

*Every*one has experienced automatic, repeating reactions to situations, events and others' behaviors. After we experience an upsetting situation, you later revisit the upsetting situation in your memories where you plan what to do better or differently the next time. But the results of the "next time" are usually not much different or satisfying.

Why can't you just tell yourselves—or each other—to act differently and then respond differently the "next time" you find yourselves in that upsetting situation, event or dealing with the person who "pushes your buttons?"

The reason is that patterns, which are responsible for those repeating, upsetting feelings and unwanted behaviors, are the sources of those automatic feelings and behaviors. And patterns lie within the unconscious, well beyond your conscious awareness and control.

Until now, everyone has been looking for a logical, rational reason why you and I act and think in ways that are counterproductive to our best intentions. However, a pattern cannot be "understood" because it operates in the irrational, illogical, brain where cause and effect have no meaning and thus cannot be "understood". You all seek to avoid "anxiety" (triggers) by avoiding situations, events and others that you know cause us to feel that anxiety. You even avoid certain upsetting thoughts, words and memories. The following section contains a category listing of what I mean by anxiety.

- Anxiety (Fears, negative thoughts, worries about "what if", what I could, should, would said or done)
- Bugged/Controlled by people who press my buttons (Children, parents, teachers, politicians, coaches, friends, co-workers)

- Bullied/Cyberbullied/Made fun of/Put down/Picked on (School, neighborhood, workplace, siblings, bosses, relationships, marriages, in-laws)
- "Character flaws" (Feeling inadequate, shame, incomplete, scarred, defective, "damaged")
- Fighting/wrestling with my demons
- Financial worries
- I'm my worst enemy/I sabotage myself
- Insecurities/Confidence issues
- Making the same mistakes I swore I'd never make again
- No matter what I do, it's never good enough/Always disappointing others

Your perceptions and reactions are determined by patterns that are inherited or formed in your childhood or later years. These patterns work in the unconscious, removed from your conscious awareness. Patterns cause internal mental chatter and compulsive behaviors.

A pattern is concerned only with its survival. It disguises its presence by causing you to project and blame its operations onto others and external conditions. A pattern will allow you to see and do only those things that do not threaten its existence.

A pattern will become stronger every time you are reacting, not responding, to a situation in which the pattern operates.

You cannot use intellectual, rational methods to analyze or control patterns. You must destroy the pattern to find relief.

You now understand the nature and operation of patterns. You are now aware of how they have directed your life. Your current awareness by itself is the crucial first step in the process of annihilating the patterns that have robbed you of the full enjoyment of your life. Your awareness guarantees that the patterns can no longer operate without interference.

As Dr. Crowley shares, awareness of the pattern comes first, then the annihilation. Trying to do either by yourself is difficult. This is usually where an executive coach like myself is brought in to uncover the patterns associated with self-sabotaging habits and help you break them. Some habits are somewhat superficial and broken easily while others are deeply ingrained and require more deliberate work to be changed.

I wasn't sure how at first a habit could be annihilated. But I remembered something that Rick Martin, one of my first coaching instructors, asked us new coaches, "Please define the word freedom." Of course he got all sorts of answers, however what he wrote down next changed my life. "True freedom is the ability between stimulus and response to pause and in that pause, choose" (Frankel 1984).

I was finalizing my divorce from my first wife and in a raw emotional state when I heard that definition. No one had ever told me I could choose how I could respond to the emotions I was experiencing at any time. My ex-wife had learned how to trigger me at any time so I felt my reactions were just natural at the time.

A fellow coach gave me a suggestion that helped me break the pattern of unconsciously responding when I was triggered. He said "Create a simple catch phrase that will get you to pause and choose how to react." "Don't bite" has become my phrase of choice. When I'm emotionally triggered and about to "lose it" I say out loud "don't bite" (not too loudly) and it gives me the mental break I need to stop the emotional hijacking and time to think on how to respond. My wife's phrase of choice is "Bingo!" We also have an agreement that if we see the other being triggered we say their catch phrase. No other words are necessary.

Dr. David Drake, in his work "Narrative Coaching," calls this moment a "Pivot point." It is a moment in time when you stop an old pattern and pivot (similar to a basketball player looking to move or pass the ball in another direction). You take a different, more effective and positive direction or response rather than the old response (Drake 2018, 253).

With practice an old response is replaced automatically with the response you choose at any given moment. I'll give you a quick example. When my wife Lisa and I got married, I suddenly had a 12-year-old step-daughter Samm living in the house. I love this child as my own, always will. However, she and I do not share the same "neatness" gene at home. Leaving her "stuff" all over the house really used to set me on edge. I learned that negotiating with a young woman on this was futile.

My wife suggested I had a choice, put the things away without getting upset or stay angry. I don't enjoy being angry, let alone at my daughter, the choice was mine and I chose not to be angry. I am glad I did.

As an adult Samm has worked at various restaurants to support her musical theater career. I've seen her in action and she is one of the hardest working, "keep it clean" employees I have ever observed. So I get it—at home she just wanted to relax and get things done in her own time. Now that she is married with her own place, I miss not having her "stuff" around.

My point is, you cannot control the stimulus, but you can control your response. I don't try to suppress the negative feeling a particular stimulus may cause; that only causes way too much internal stress for me. Rather, I take a moment, breathe, let it pass, and then determine what I am going to say or do next. That course of action rather than reacting is much more satisfying in the end.

Last thoughts on patterns for now. When it comes to breaking patterns or habits I've heard the same excuse over and over "I can't stop or break the habit, I'm hard wired that way" or "It's just who I am, I can't change that." Not true, in fact just the opposite is possible and happens all the time. It is correct that your DNA will not change from birth, your height, eye color, gender, skin color, natural hair color, and so on is hard wired. However your brain is not coded that way.

Research has determine our brains have a plasticity to them, new pathways are formed when we learn new things, develop new physical skills, and adapt to new surrounding and people. New pathways are formed each time you break a habit or old pattern of behavior. You are not locked into or "hard wired" to behave or respond to things the same way forever (Grodnitzky 2014, 12).

Trust Builder #8—Taking Action

There are very few things that solidify trust faster than you taking positive action. It is the visible sign of you following through on what you say you are going to do. Being verbally well-intentioned doesn't count. Your lack of action causes doubt around your ability to lead and doubt kills trust.

Everyone has doubts at times. It can stem from a lack of confidence in yourselves or in others. Doubt creates a negative state of mind, leading you to create all sorts of stories and scenarios around negative outcomes. Doubt is often synonymous with distrust because the feelings you get are so similar. Doubt interferes with your ability in taking action—you pause, you procrastinate, and you overthink what you need to do, doubt kills the warrior spirit.

Again, do not commit to anything unless you have every intention of following through. Be strong enough to set boundaries and learn to say "no" rather than over-commit. Personal integrity demands that you give every task your best. The results may not be perfect, but so what? Giving any task 100 percent is more important than the planned result. Are you more or less inclined to be in a trusting relationship with someone who is always willing to give any task their best shot? This doesn't mean that you expect them to do things far beyond their competence or skill set. But it does mean setting the right expectations for all concerned to create a win-win situation.

I know this is a long chapter with a lot to digest. Take the time to reflect on all the things you have read about killing and building trust. You will need all of it when working on your business.

Thoughts for Reflection

- How comfortable are you with emotions, yours or others?
- Are you conservative in showing your emotions or do you wear your heart on your sleeve?
- Can you envision yourself as vulnerable, strong and safe at the same time?
- How much importance do you place on other people's perception of you?
- How quick are you to rush to judgment about people or situations?
- How often do you make assumptions rather than ask questions?
- Do you procrastinate or take action on things you feel are unpleasant or don't like to do?

- Do you take the time to listen to others or dismiss them quickly if you disagree?
- How often do you have to be right?
- What was the last old pattern of behavior you changed?
- What was the last new habit you formed and why?

CHAPTER 8

Confidence, Competence, and Trust

Earlier in my book I had noted one author's definition of trust as "trust equals confidence." While trust and confidence are interconnected they are not the same and it is very important, especially as a CEO to know the difference. There are many recent examples of individuals who had supreme confidence in themselves that became arrogance. They also were highly competent in their respective industries, becoming well known and well paid. The combination of over-confidence and high competence can breed almost a god-like mindset, they are untouchable and highly untrustworthy. The Enron scandal had just taken place and became a big topic of discussion in my MBA ethics course. The abuse of the trust placed in founder Ken Lay and CEO Jeff Skilling was staggering. Not only did they scam their consumers and stock holders, thousands of innocent employees lost their jobs as well. The report of their personal spending habits reached epic proportions.

Bill Cosby and Harvey Weinstein both had high confidence and competence in acting and making movies respectively. The combination became arrogance where they believed they were above the law and could use their power and money to abuse and degrade women who came to them for help with their careers.

As a CEO, it is important to understand the differences between confidence, competence, and trust, for you and assessing your employees. Confidence is the belief that you are good at something, either a mental skill, a physical skill or both. Your confidence rises and falls based on your perception of your ability to do well in the given situation. Competence is the actual mental or physical skill of being capable of doing the task at hand. Competence is usually gained through study, repetition, trial and error, and any combination thereof. Competence is judged on how well you perform any given task.

Trust, however, is different. In the workplace trust is built upon your belief that an employee will:

- Do what they say they will do, accurately and on time.
- Will admit if they don't have the confidence or competence to do something.
- Admit and own their mistakes because they overestimated their competence.
- Not take credit for another employee's competence.
- Have the confidence to step up their game as the company need arises.

I am sure you can add to this list. The point however is that trust is not interchangeable with the other two, and this understanding can completely change the context of your working relationships.

The Job Description

Job descriptions include all of the duties, responsibilities, and skill sets an employer requires for a particular position. All manner of assessments have been created and used to determine a particular candidate's success in that position. What is generally not tested or determined by an interview is trustworthiness or other character attributes.

Imagine for a moment a job description that started off like this: All candidates for this position must:

- Be trustworthy, you cannot lie, steal, take credit for co-workers work or sabotage their work to further your career.
- Work well with others and own their success, everyone wins or loses together in this company.
- Take pride, own your work and not blame others for things that were within your control.
- Admit your mistakes and take ownership of the solution, no excuses. Admit when you don't know how to do something and immediately ask for help.

- Be willing to learn new skills as this company and your job evolves over time.
- Be a mature adult and treat all co-workers as adults, with respect for them and their contribution to your success.
- Will not participate in gossiping, bullying or being intolerant of the things that make each employee unique.

I'm sure you get the idea of where I am going with this. Employers hire for those with competent skills and past experience but rarely for mindset or behavioral attributes. Does this list sound far-fetched? It's not, I just paraphrased part of the mindset required to become a Navy Seal. It is the mindset and mental preparation that enables a soldier to pass the grueling Seal boot camp, only 10 percent make it. The real Seal training only begins after you pass. If you want to bring a culture of trust into your business you have to start by hiring people with the right attitudes and behaviors.

The CEO Dilemmas

Several years ago I was referred to a CEO who ran a large distribution company. George was a successful CEO running a growing national business and he had a dilemma. George had received complaints about his top salesperson Rick from co-workers and support staff, that this individual had become arrogant, abusive and blamed everyone else when a sale fell through. George also suspected he was cutting his own side deals or getting kick-backs from some supplies to push their products ahead of others.

George approached Rick about these issues and Rick blamed his co-workers for being jealous that he closed more deals and made more commission than them. He had to be tough with his support staff in order to get the sales and keep the clients happy. They were a bunch of "crybabies" and not to be taken seriously. George let it go for the time being.

However, the complaints continued and several support staff left, they could not work with Rick. George approached Rick again with the same issues. This time Rick's answer was blunt "If you are not happy with my work there are several of our competitors who would love to have me. I'm a great salesperson, just let me do my job." George was taken aback and had to stop and assess the situation. Rick was the top salesperson bringing in almost 20 percent of the top line sales. He could not afford to have Rick go to a competitor and lose all this business.

So he tolerated the behavior until his second and third top salespeople left taking some valuable clients with them. It was at this time George came to me, perplexed and not sure of his next step. George still had a relationship with the salespeople who left so I suggest he meet with them to find out why they left. He did, but was flabbergasted by what they had to say.

They told George they used to hold him in high regard as a man of principle who built a great business. But after watching him tolerate Rick's abysmal behavior they doubted his ability to make good decisions. They were concerned that the company was then heading in the wrong direction and it was time for them to go. George defended his position to them because the business couldn't afford to lose Rick's sales. The two salespeople said "that's the point George, you assumed the clients would leave because they belonged to Rick and not the company. Those clients want to do business with us because we can deliver what they need when they need it. I'll bet most of those clients tolerate Rick the same way you do because they don't feel they have a choice like you don't feel you have a choice." Ouch. George had allowed his perception of Rick's confidence and competence to over-ride his better judgment.

After I left his office he called Rick who was on the road to have him come in the next day. When Rick arrived he was promptly let go. George made an apology to his support staff for not listening to them and tolerating Rick's poor behavior for so long. He then called his two former top salespeople and apologized to them as well for not being strong enough to let Rich go when he knew it was the right thing to do. He asked them to come back and they agreed to do so providing the George they knew was back. He assured them he wouldn't fall into that trap again.

Rick was right, he did get hired by a competitor right away and proceeded to call on his old clients. He was going to show George that he had made a mistake in firing him. Only two clients left George and the rest stayed. Not only did they stay but George's sales from them rose dramatically. The cancer had been removed and the company healed. Rick's new employer was very unhappy that all the clients Rick promised to bring with him never materialized. Rick was back out on the street within a year and out of the industry shortly thereafter.

I wish I could say this type of ending happens all the time, it doesn't. Sometimes the company never heals after the cancer is gone, or a new cancer grows to fill the void after the old one left. What do you do when the toxic employee has a particular expertise or skillset that you need? In reality Rick's perceived competence and confidence were smoke and mirrors, he talked a good game. George let his fear override his trust in ability to make good decisions.

I am not suggesting the choices in these situations are easy, they are not. I'll talk more about having to make tough decisions in the last part of this book.

The Right Words Make All the Difference

I'll give you a quick example of the importance of not confusing competence, confidence, and trust using employee feedback. Using the appropriate words in assessing performance can make all the difference in the world. This is the simplified conversation I had with a manager I was coaching because he was struggling to provide accurate feedback to his direct reports. Jack is the manager and Steve is one of his direct reports.

Jack said to me, "I told Steve I trusted him to deliver his reports on time but that I didn't always trust his accuracy. Steve got confused and then upset, I don't understand why he got so upset." I asked Jack why he used the word trust, it sends a harsh message when you tell someone you don't trust them. I asked Jack how he would feel if his boss told him he was untrustworthy. Jack said "No that's what I mean, Steve is very trustworthy, straight as they come, but his work is sometimes inaccurate."

I asked Jack to rephrase his same sentence using the words "confidence" and "competence" instead of trust. "I am confident in Steve's ability to deliver his reports on time but he appears to lack competence in his accuracy." Trust was never the issue, accuracy of the reports was the problem. Now Jack can have a very different conversation with Steve about how to improve the accuracy of his reports.

This is one example of how certain words, especially the word trust, cannot be used interchangeably. Trust is a very powerful word, use it carefully because it immediately engages emotions and not always in the way you intend. I'm also going to say that robust vocabulary is a real plus for being able to articulate what you are thinking or feeling at any time.

Implicit Trust at Work

I'm going to end this chapter with a few industries we rely on and give implicit trust without question or hesitation. Even though there is a risk of injury or death we assume the people involved know what they are doing and don't ask for credentials.

The airlines, including airline pilots, plane manufacturers, plane mechanics, and air traffic controllers, you put your life in their hands every time you get onto a plane. Doctors, surgeons, nurses, and other medical professionals, you trust them to heal you when you are sick. If you ever had to dial 911, did you not trust that the responders knew what they were doing? After 20 years as an EMT and Fire Fighter I can safely tell you that all the 911 caller wants to know is that you can help them, no questions asked.

Most businesses however are not given that implicit trust and have to work on cultivating it with staff and all your stakeholders. That's ok, by the end of this book you will know how to create and sustain that depth of trust.

Thoughts for Reflection

- Have you ever confused trust with confidence or competence with an employee?
- Have you defined the attributes you want for each employee before defining the job description?
- Which comes first, confidence or competence?
- At what point does confidence become arrogance?
- Have you ever hired for competence only to fire for attitude and behavior?

CHAPTER 9

The Vulnerability Scale and the Trust Matrix

Each of you have an internal scale that you use to determine how vulnerable you are willing to be in any given situation. For some people, this scale pegs over to full trust quite easily; for others, the needle never seems to move past cautious or suspicious. For the rest of us, the needle moves back and forth all the time.

I've created the scale in Figure 9.1 to illustrate this point. The scale ranges from zero trust (paranoia) all the way over to intimacy (surrender). None of your feelings will be absolute or purely black and white, so the points on the scale are unique to you.

You move your needle intuitively up and down on the scale depending on what you are feeling. The needle placement on your scale is totally subjective; no two people will react the same way to any type of stimulus. Mixed feelings may cause your needle to bounce around quite a bit as you wrestle with an issue. Other times your fears or desires can easily override where your intuition is telling you to go on the scale. Moving your needle to the most effective amount of vulnerability takes practice, thought, and

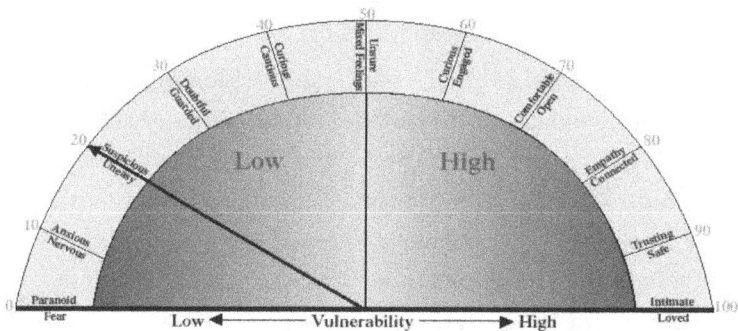

Figure 9.1 Vulnerability scale

reflection. It also requires setting boundaries between the points on the scale and what it will take to move beyond that boundary.

Setting boundaries on who to trust, how much, and when is one of the key purposes behind this scale. Your core values and personal standards place a key role in setting the demarcation points on the scale. Looking at the scale, what would it take in a working relationship to move the needle past 60 (curious) to 70 (comfortable)? Pick one relationship you have now that you would like to improve the level of trust between you and write it down. You will use it in the next section.

Once you are clear in your mind how to set boundaries, you will be able to use this scale with the utmost confidence. After that, you will be able to determine how to improve the level of trust with all the key people and roles within your organization.

Building Your Personal Vulnerability Scale

You can construct virtually any type of scale you want that makes sense to you. My illustration is just one example. It is a simple model, can be used in many ways, and is easy to visualize. After 20 years of facilitating meetings I have found simple graphics are the easiest to use and be remembered long term. Keep this in mind as you will be using a scale with others in your organization for defining the boundaries for each level of trust required at each level in your organization. Building your own scale first makes it much easier to discuss the concept with others going forward. For your personal trust scale to work effectively, several things need to occur:

- Being aware that you have a scale and making the decision to consciously use it.
- Calibrate the scale by reflecting on the decisions you have made in setting boundaries. Was I too vulnerable or not vulnerable enough to be effective?
- Understand that you will be biased toward those who appear to have similar core values. Just because you like or feel comfortable with someone does not mean you do not have to set appropriate boundaries.
- Be very clear about the differences between trust, confidence, and core competence.

- Don't rush to judgment; be careful of quick thinking assumptive action. Be deliberate in setting your boundaries.
- Constantly refine and recalibrate your scale when you know you have made a poor decision. Don't justify the decision, learn from it.

Calibrate Your Scale Using Your Core Values

Calibrating your scale is a constant process. New people and situations will arise all the time to challenge the boundaries you set along your scale. Some situations will expose flaws in where or how you set the demarcation points along your scale; other choices and experiences will reinforce why you drew the boundary line where you did. I'll give you an example that I hope clarifies this scale. My client Elaine confided she was tired and upset by co-workers and upper management constantly taking advantage of her good nature. It was getting to the point where she was not getting her own work done on time and that bothered her greatly. She said, "I like people and enjoy working with others and I want to be liked by them in return so we can all get along. But now I can't finish my own work on time!"

Elaine's default position on the scale was somewhere between 70 (Open) and 80 (Connected) for everything. She equated that position to being liked and set no boundaries around that position. As a result, two things were happening: first, her co-workers and managers just saw her as someone who never said "no" or "not now" to anything they asked her to do, so why stop asking? Second, her desire to be liked prevented her from saying no out of fear of damaging her relationship or upsetting the status quo. She didn't understand she could say no to taking on additional work and preserve her default position of openness and connection.

We worked on setting boundaries by establishing the fact that her time was just as valuable as others. If she didn't respect that value, no one else would. Here is where clarity of core values is very useful in setting effective boundaries and keeping them. Her desire to be liked was overriding her value of integrity—living up to her word.

I've already discussed how clarity of core values polishes your lens. This concept holds true for your organization as well. Without clearly defined corporate values, your strengths, weakness, opportunities, and threats may not be as recognizable as they should be. Additionally, a culture of low vulnerability and distrust will not accommodate the types of conversations necessary to leverage those strengths and diminish the weaknesses.

Your words and actions just as your company's communication and service must be in alignment with your core values, otherwise something is out of whack. Think back to Enron or Wells Fargo. Their core values were merely a front to hide the real actions taking place behind closed doors. Their unethical actions cost thousands of stakeholders millions of dollars in lost investments, wages, pensions, and jobs.

Anything you perceive as violating a core value on your scale should automatically put moving the needle on hold. All questions and actions must be satisfactorily examined and answered before the needle can be moved at all. I will discuss in another chapter a process by which your company can make quick assessments and move on in most cases.

Just a reminder from the last chapter: don't confuse confidence, competence, and trust! As I said earlier, there are many examples of individuals with high confidence, high competence, and extremely low moral standards. It is for those reasons I do not have those factored competence and confidence into the vulnerability scale.

Recalibrate Your Boundaries Regularly

Reflecting on what worked and what didn't for the important decisions you make is all part of honing your boundaries. Reflection is a time to pause and think about a decision made and the action taken. Why is this important? More is learned by studying failures than from success stories. The military will spend two hours briefing on how a mission is to be accomplished and eight hours going over the details after the mission is over. The goal is to reinforce positive thinking by learning from the mistakes.

Reflection is not a time for self-recrimination or beat yourself up over past mistakes. Human beings, it seems, are the only creatures on this planet who will beat themselves up over and over again for a single mistake. The best leaders learn from their mistakes and bounce back quickly to keep leading. Now let's use the boundaries on your vulnerability scale to create the trust matrix for your business.

Creating the Trust Matrix

I've built a simple matrix for using the trust scale numbers 1 to 100 (see Table 9.1). Across the top of the matrix are the names of people (changed to protect them) on a team I worked with. Each person is graded on the vulnerability scale by using the format of sentence completion (Branden 1998). Each sentence is based on a core value of the company; each value is listed by the associated question. Each sentence can be tailored to the core values of the company or another standard. This particular list was

Table 9.1 Trust matrix

Score each of the people using a scale of 1 to 100 1 being complete distrust and 100 being absolute trust by completing the following sentences:					
I trust <u>Name</u> to:	Core Value(s)	Bill	Tom	Sue	Roger
1. Do what they say they're going to do	Integrity, Competence Discipline, Persistence	85	80	35	80
2. Respect others	Respect	50	85	55	65
3. Tell the truth	Honesty	30	80	35	65
4. Ask for help when need it	Courage	20	60	45	55
5. Admit when they do not know something	Honesty, Courage	5	60	45	40
6. Keep confidential information confidential	Integrity	20	60	35	65
7. Not use confidential information against me	Honesty, Integrity	25	80	5	70
8. Respect my thoughts and opinions	Integrity, Tolerance Equality, Fairness	10	60	20	60
9. Be on time for meetings	Respect, Integrity Accountability, Commitment	40	80	30	30
10. Respect my time	Respect	20	65	30	30
11. Respect my feelings	Respect	20	60	30	70
12. Not gossip	Truth, Support, Teamwork	30	40	40	30
13. Not blame others for their mistakes	Honesty, Integrity, Courage	20	35	55	45
14. Always do their best	Excellence	35	35	65	60
Total Score out of 1,400 points		410	880	525	765
Average		30%	63%	38%	55%

developed for building trust in this specific group who desired to create more of a team mindset. However, it can easily be used for all the people in your organization and adapted for most business situations.

Words of caution: The number assigned to each sentence by the person completing the form is completely subjective. It is their perspective and theirs alone. The matrix is not designed to pass judgment and determine if someone is "good or bad." Be careful, any tool used improperly can cause more harm than good. Keep the numbers simple. I have seen some organizations go out three decimal points trying to be more "accurate." Perceptions and emotions don't work that way; they are rarely logical with clearly defined boundaries.

The matrix is designed to be a visual display of what you are doing internally and creating a starting point for conversation. Effective conversation is critically important for developing trust and leading to higher vulnerability. I will talk more about conversations to create trust in the next chapters.

It is obvious in the example matrix that the group member completing the sentences has the strongest sense of trust with Tom, slightly less with Roger, and very little with Bill or Sue. The numbers are not right or wrong; they just represent the experience this individual has had with each person. In this case all five individuals completed the matrix for each other with interesting results. Bill rated low with everyone, at least 35 percent or lower. Tom scored much higher with the group with a combined average score of 73 percent. The scores of Sue and Roger were all over the place with no apparent reason. None of the sentence completions had the same or even close scores. However, subsequent conversations uncovered that several deeply rooted misunderstandings going back over two years led to those scores. Even though the projects and goals had changed several times for this group, the underlying distrust had not gone away.

Once the old issues were uncovered the group members were able to air their grievances and make amends and agreed to move forward by not allowing issues to fester and be more open with their conversations. We also created a "self-righting" mechanism for this group to help them get back on track if anyone feels the group trust is being eroded. Self-righting is a nautical term used to describe why a boat on the water does not roll over and capsize in heavy seas. You can find that process in the Trust Factor Workbook.

If Only They Would

Once the matrix is created for each person involved, the next phase is identifying what it would take for the other person to say or do to move the needle on your scale. Remember: this is subjective on your part, and designed to open conversation rather than be a character assassination of the other person(s). This is another reason why I feel it is so important to have everyone involved read the book first and be on the same page before starting any of this work. You have no idea what may be uncovered during this process.

The "If Only They Would" section is completed prior to the group meeting and requires you to write down the specific instances that caused you to assign the number you did to each sentence for each person. The specifics must be first person (no gossip or hearsay), factual, and as specific as possible. I'll give you an example of this using the first sentence for Sue who scored a 30 on her team leader Mary's trust matrix.

Mary wrote, "If only Sue would do what she says she is going to do. Every week she tells me she is going to complete her expense report accurately and turn it in on time. Every week her report is late, full of mistakes and I constantly have to ask her to redo it. That's the reason I gave her a 30. I just don't trust her to do what she says she will do." I know this sounds a bit simplistic, but I can tell from experience this happens all the time.

Safe space must be created in order to allow constructive conversations to happen after the written work is done. In this space there can be no judgment, embarrassment, retribution, or fear of reprisal from anyone. I've actually posted this vulnerability scale diagram on the wall and asked each person to draw the needle on the diagram as to how safe they feel prior to starting the meeting. Unless everyone is well over a score of 50, don't continue. First determine what it would take to move the needle to at least that score or higher.

Once you reach that point the next step is to create what are called the "Rules of Engagement" for how we as a group are going to conduct ourselves in a meeting. Here is a brief list of some rules from other groups:

- Be on time for every meeting—respect each other's time.
- Meetings will begin and end on time—respect the group's time.

- Be prepared for the meeting—honor your commitments.
- Don't interrupt anyone when they are speaking.
- Challenge assumptions but be respectful.
- Don't answer for someone if they are being quiet while thinking of an answer to a question.
- Don't ask multiple questions; let the other person answer one question before asking the next.

You will find that your meetings are more enjoyable and productive by laying this groundwork before starting. You can find out more about "Rules of Engagement" in the workbook as well. With that work being done, next came the tough questions and the conversations that most of the group had been avoiding.

"What was Sue's reason for always being late with her reports?"

"Why do you constantly accept the fact she is always late? This holds all of us up from getting reimbursed for our expenses."

"I didn't know that's why we are always late in getting our reimbursements, how come I'm only hearing about this now?"

After about an hour of "lively" conversation, the group realized that this and many other issues had not come out for two important reasons: the first was none of them felt safe enough to complain to Mary about the issue and second, they didn't know how to get a difficult conversation started. It finally came out that Sue was getting pulled in all directions with work coming in from her group and people outside her group; she was completely overwhelmed. Sue, like Elaine in my past example, was a real people pleaser and didn't want to disappoint anyone by telling them she couldn't do what needed to be done on time. It didn't take long to uncover a whole host of misunderstandings, fears of letting others down, being overwhelmed, and too embarrassed to ask for help.

It took almost a whole day for these five people to get through each individual trust matrix; there were some very tense moments and not everything turned out well. As group leader, Mary realized she had not taken ownership of the group's success and had allowed the group members to disconnect from each other. She also had to think hard on why those in her group did not feel safe enough to express how they felt about their working relationships.

Bill on the other hand took real offense at being rated so poorly by the others. He was hurt, upset, and ultimately left the group for another job within the company. Unfortunately for him, the group he joined was much quicker to point out he was not carrying his weight and he soon left the company. Without Bill in the group, the whole context changed and I will share later on the tools I gave them to have much more effective, meaningful conversations. I also gave them an earlier version of the self-righting tool in the workbook to help them keep on track and not let issues fester.

When Not to Trust

One final point on this before I move on. I have made some very poor choices in my life as to whom I thought I could trust. As I mentioned early in this book, I entered into a business relationship with someone who I had no tangible reason to trust. I had become a victim to the business and personal stress I was under, allowing me to make the assumption he was trustworthy rather than digging deep into his background. It was only after his ruthless behavior toward me and my family that others came forward to share their personal knowledge of his past horrible treatment of other people and underhanded business dealings. Former businesses associates from Florida to California called to see how I was doing. One old acquaintance said, "Russ, if I had to make my money the way he made his, I'd rather be a bum on skid row." Not much I could add to that.

The moral of the story is: no matter what the circumstances, the level of stress you are under or the lure of achieving a dream should never prevent you from doing exhaustive due diligence on the trustworthiness of someone you are going to enter into an important relationship. The stakes will be too high and the risk too great not to do so. As I said earlier my grandfather told me a person's true colors or true character (or lack thereof) should be taken very seriously.

There is a Russian fable called "The Scorpion and the Frog," and I use this story to highlight the concept of "true colors." According to the fable a frog is sitting by the edge of a river enjoying his day. Along comes a scorpion who asks the frog to carry him across a river. The frog declines and says, "You are a scorpion, you will sting me and I will die."

But the scorpion argues, "If I did that, I would die too, as we both will drown." The frog considers this a sensible argument and agrees to transport the scorpion on his back across the river. The scorpion climbs onto the frog's back and the frog begins to swim. However, midway across the river the scorpion stings the frog, dooming them both. The dying frog asks the scorpion why it stung him, to which the scorpion replies, "I'm a scorpion—it's what we do."

Expecting someone else to change their behavior and move into a more trusting relationship is not always possible. It may be what you want from them, but they may not be able to do so. This happens quite often at work. Some job responsibilities require higher levels of trust than the person in that position can do. Even more so in a virtual workforce. What do you do? Going back to the earlier example of the CEO and his top salesperson, sometimes the tough choice has to be made to change the people rather than risking violating the trust.

There is no negotiation on the corporate core values; a job's roles, responsibilities, and scope of authority must be aligned with those values. I will talk more about that in the next chapter. For now, take the time to become very clear on the importance of defining your scale, setting boundaries on the expectations of trust at each mark along the scale, and how it might apply to your business.

Thoughts for Reflection

- Where along the scale do you feel is your normal default position when it comes to being vulnerable?
- Have you ever created a mental "If only they would" list about someone but never shared it with them?
- How do you currently start a difficult or uncomfortable conversation?
- Do you assume employees are appropriately trustworthy without understanding what is required in their role in the company?

CHAPTER 10

Roles, Responsibilities, and Scope of Authority

Now, let's dig deeper into your business. Regardless of the type of organizational structure there are a few common elements for every business owner and CEO that are crucial for you to get the results you want. I'll start off with Dr. Deming's quote again as it bears repeating: "Every system is perfectly designed to get the results it gets." You already have a corporate structure, employees, and processes in place. If you are getting exactly the results you want that's great. If not, don't expect different results without making important changes, especially in your corporate culture.

I spent two years getting my MBA in organizational development and leading change. The course work covered a lot of important material and there was one aspect piece that stuck out in my mind because very few CEOs had it well defined. That was the *scope of authority*.

When you look at an organizational chart of a business, the roles and responsibilities are broken down into one type of hierarchy or another. Each position on the organizational chart is designed to create and capture value all along the value chain (how your company makes a profit). The role is typically titled (CEO, CFO, COO, CMO, and so on) and lets each employee know where they fit into the overall structure. The responsibilities are then defined for that role so each knows what they are supposed to do on a daily basis to help all of the other employees achieve the corporate goals. When an organizational chart is done well, none of the roles or responsibilities overlap. There are also no gaps between the roles and each person in your organization knows who they report to, who their peer is, and who reports to them. Right?

There is on crucial piece that is often missing, the scope of their authority. Their authority dictates the parameter in which they can make decisions, spend money, take risks, and fully execute their responsibilities without having to ask another person. Close your eyes for a second and mentally look at each of your direct reports and their direct reports. Is the authority for each one of these important people clearly spelled out and written down? If so, you are well ahead of the game. If not, I will cover this topic in more detail shortly.

I bring up these three parts, roles, responsibilities, and scope of authority, in the organizational chart because they tend to be common to all businesses and more importantly this is where bonds of trust create efficiently throughout your business.

Roles and Responsibilities

I spoke earlier about the general nature of job descriptions and what they might look like if attributes, attitudes, and core values desired for a position were expressed first and the skill set secondary. The old adage about hiring is that "Businesses often hire for skills and fire for behavior." Think back a minute to the CEO I mentioned who kept a supposedly top-performing salesperson (his role and responsibility) to the company's detriment. The salesperson's behavior and attitude were toxic to the other employees.

I think one of the reasons that Navy Seals are kept in high regard is the ruthless mental and physical testing and assessment of a candidate's attitude and behaviors before any high-level skills are taught. The Seals do not assume potential candidates have the core values and mental attitudes they will need to succeed. The stakes are too high.

Given two candidates for your business, which would you want: one has high skill test scores but lower behavioral scores, the other has high behavioral scores and slightly lower skill test scores? Take it a step further, which one do you think will grow and thrive under the demands of the work and who will break under stress? I'll let you decide. Take stock of your company. Do you as a leader and your organization on the whole have the culture that will attract the first candidate above or the second? I've seen behind the curtain of businesses voted "Best Place to Work" and quite often they are not. If I polled all of your employees on a scale of 1 to 100 based on:

- clearly defined and vigorously followed core values;
- feeling that you are appreciated and respected;
- your role, responsibility, and scope of authority within the company is well defined;
- you are allowed to exercise your authority without being micromanaged; and
- your ideas and suggestions for improvement are taken seriously,

how would your company fare in this assessment? It is not a comprehensive list by any means and I purposely left out compensation. I am a firm believer that really successful companies perform effective 360 assessments (growth orientated, not punitive) in one form or another with their employees and for the company on a regular basis to keep everyone on track.

Scope of Authority

In Chapter 1, I mentioned briefly the stress and loss of productivity caused by not defining the scope of authority for each role in your company. Authority is not often discussed and many of the companies that I have either worked with or researched do not have it written down as part of the individual's job outline. A set of responsibilities is defined for each role with the intention that at least one person touches each transaction as it moves through the company and nothing falls between the boxes on the chart. However, what is often missing is the scope of authority necessary for each person in your organization to effectively carry out their responsibilities. I'll give you a quick story to highlight what I mean by scope of authority. A while ago I was traveling cross country on business. Poor weather caused flights to be delayed and connecting flights missed. If this has happened to you, then you understand how I was feeling by the time I finally reached my hotel long after I was supposed to check in.

All day long I heard airline personnel telling unhappy travelers there was nothing they could do to help, bad weather, cancelled flights, local hotels overbooked, and so on. One of the biggest complaints by weary travelers was the lack of communication by staff on what could be done and it appeared no one on the front line had the authority to do anything other than say the situation was out of their control.

I was expecting the same problem at the hotel, but I was very wrong. I was supposed to check in around 4 p.m. and it was then 2 a.m. the next day. Stan at the front desk greeted me. He already knew I would be late because my flight had been delayed due to bad weather. No problem, each of the people at the front desk of this hotel have the authority to immediately accept late arrivals and if possible upgrade rooms as available to make up for their guests' horrible travel day. He told me my room was ready and wanted to know what I needed to be prepared for my business meeting in six hours. The bellboy took my bag to the room and took my suit and shirt to be pressed; he had the authority to put a rush on it, no questions asked. Breakfast was ordered and to be delivered to my room as I would not have time for their normal breakfast hours. I went to sleep feeling well taken care of and certainly less anxious about being ready for my meeting in a few hours.

I've never forgotten that experience and none of the employees had to ask what to do or get permission. They went about their business as if each person was an owner. Their expressed authority empowered them by giving them ownership of any given situation. I felt great and I could tell the staff thoroughly enjoyed being able to take action as needed to do their job well. They felt trusted! The scope of authority sets the boundaries of where authority over people, process, and resources begins and also where it ends. The scope of authority should include the following elements when applicable:

- Decision-making authority, restrictions, and ethical responsibility
- Financial authorizations, restrictions, and allocation of resources
- Reporting requirements—who do I report to and who reports to me
- What you are personally responsible for doing and what can be delegated to others
- Who you can delegate to and under what circumstances
- Process for communication and the chain of command

- Social media policy and external PR
- Plan for ongoing project evaluations and who and when can authorize changes

This is not an all-inclusive list and should be tailored to your company-specific roles and processes. Decision making is critical to your company's success, and so many companies get bogged down in the smaller routine decisions that are made on a daily basis. Clearly defined scopes of authority dramatically remove confusion and allow employees to exercise their authority constructively. There are basic standards for authority within a business structure and this is a compilation of what I have seen in the various businesses I have coached or consulted.

- Level One: No authority at all, wait to be told what to do, how to do it, when to do it and do exactly as requested without deviation.
- Level Two: Ask me first before you make any decisions. I may or may not let you decide what to do.
- Level Three: You get to make the decision but talk to me first before you do anything. This is not the same as Level Two. It is agreed ahead of time what the employee will be able to decide.
- Level Four: The employee has the authority to make the decision and then inform you of the decision and action taken.
- Level Five: The employee has the authority to make the decision and then inform you of the decision and action taken at a later date or in a weekly, monthly, or quarterly report.
- Level Six: The employee has the authority to make the decision; there is no need to inform you.
- Level Seven: That's you as the CEO, president, or business owner. Yours is the ultimate authority.

The scope and level of authority should increase as you get higher in your organization. Each level comes with a much higher degree of responsibility. However, trust is multidirectional, meaning it works up, down, and across each level of the organization. Those in upper management trust all those who report to them are doing what they are supposed to do without them micromanaging. Those who report up must trust their leadership is making decisions for everyone's benefit, not just their own. Trust across the organization breaks down barriers to ineffective communication and working in silos. I emphasize trust within the scope of authority because this is where important decisions are made and abiding by core values becomes critically necessary. I'll give you an example of one of my favorite companies that embodies this methodology and then show you how they incorporate these three things with culture and leadership discussed in the next chapter.

Clif Bars was founded in 1990 by Gary Erickson who named the company after his father Clifford who taught him a love of the outdoors. As an avid outdoorsman Gary could not find trail food or energy snack that tasted good to him, so he took his baking skills and created the Clif Bar. The company culture is founded on five aspirations:

- Sustaining our Business—Building a healthy, resilient company means that we can invest in the long term, be a catalyst for change, and do more good in the world.
- Sustaining our Brands—Creating brands with integrity, quality, and authenticity means crafting good food from sustainably sourced ingredients.
- Sustaining our People—Being family-and employee-owned means taking care of our people, working side by side, and encouraging each other. Our company is our people.
- Sustaining our Communities—Promoting and supporting sustainable communities both locally and globally means making a difference where we work, source, and play.
- Sustaining the Planet—Conserving and restoring our natural resources means growing a business that operates in harmony with the laws of nature. (Clif Bar 2020)

Lofty aspirations, you bet, and for the last 20 years they have grown at least 17 percent a year and are now valued at somewhere between $500MM and $1B. Their employee turnover is less than 2 percent annually (Lagaorio 2018). Each employee is connected and has a very clear understanding of their role, responsibility, and the authority they have to execute their responsibilities. The social proof is in the company's growth, adherence to their aspirations, and very low employee turnover. In the *Trust Factor Workbook* you will find a sample organizational chart with the roles, responsibilities, and scope of authority completed for a sample company.

Thoughts for Reflection

- Are the roles, responsibilities, and scope of authority clearly defined for each position in your organization?
- How often do you look at your organizational chart and update each of those three important aspects for each role?
- How well do you delegate responsibilities and authority to others?
- What was the last thing you should have delegated that you didn't?
- Would a 360 assessment reveal that your employees feel trusted and empowered to do a great job in their respective roles?
- Do you have the aspirations for your business and stakeholders spelled out?

PART III

Creating a Culture of Trust—Safe Space and Co-Creative

CHAPTER 11

Making Choices: Culture and Leadership

One of the biggest challenges any business owner has is taking valuable written information and implementing a plan of action. As David Sadler, the creator of the Sandler Sales System, once said: "You can't teach someone how to ride a bike in a seminar." The first step in taking action starts by making some important conscious decisions. The choices you make will then determine each next step to be accomplished. Those decisions will require you to forsake other choices; in this case not all roads lead to Rome.

Culture

Creating a culture of trust in your business has to lead somewhere. First, that means making a choice on the type of culture you want. There is already extensive research available on the positive impact a healthy aligned culture has on employee morale and overall profitability (Grodnitzky 2014). I mentioned in the introduction, the shift away from corporate capitalism toward social capitalism. The traditional corporate culture does not fit well with the social capitalistic model. The end goals for corporate and socialistic companies are different and the alignment of people and process has to be different. I am a baby-boomer and grew up with a very clear sense of corporate capitalism when I started working in my family's business. I come from a long line of men and women who worked diligently in that type of corporate structure and there was not much thought of doing business any other way. I never understood I had a choice, and a culture like Clif Bar would have never entered my mind.

Current and future generations of workers want a choice, they do not want to be as compliant, and their work life balance alignment is different than prior generations. They want more social engagement. Look at the growth of use of LinkedIn, Facebook, and YouTube for business. The social proof is there; everyone wants to be connected but it has to be on their terms. There is a real downside I believe to all this connectedness. Without a sense of trust and respect, I see so many connections devolving into distrust, unfriending, social tirades, online bullying, trolls, and other toxic forms of social behavior. Here is where you can build and leverage a culture of trust to make the most positive use of social connections. Social platforms now allow you to connect with all your stakeholders in ways that were impossible to imagine before.

I believed that the culture of my business was predetermined; now I know there is a choice and you will have to decide the type of culture you want to cultivate. What type of culture do you believe will attract the best and the brightest from each new generation entering the workforce and specifically for your industry? I believe the financial numbers bear out that social capitalistic companies will outperform the older traditional corporate model. The balance of this book will be using a social capital culture as the baseline for instilling trust as the main underlying theme for everything you do.

Leadership

There are thousands of books written on leadership and leadership styles. I have already referenced a few of the ones I've researched for my book. Most of us are very familiar with the heroic model, the CEO or president leading the company. He or she is the visionary, setting the course, giving commands, and navigating the company to its goals (Goleman, Boyatzis, and McKee 2002). Some heroic leaders are charismatic like former President Bill Clinton, others tough and brooding like Apple CEO Steve Jobs, visionaries like Martin Luther King, or commanding like Jack Welch. The heroic style is more "I" centric, focusing on the individual rather than the collective group. History is full of heroic business leaders, but that style is becoming more old school; it's changing and focusing on how decisions can be made differently.

Enter in the concept of shared leadership, a more dynamic group process driven to empower all rather than just a few in the C-Suite.

The concept has been around since the 1920s and a few companies like Gore have embraced this style of leadership from the start. Others are starting to see the real benefit as the pace and complexity of business speeds up. This style fits well with the social capitalistic culture which is designed to be more inclusive of all stakeholders. We all win or lose together rather than the C-Suite getting compensation regardless of performance. There are countless examples of that scenario.

I've experienced both styles as a worker and I have been both types of leaders. In many ways the heroic model is easier because most of us are quite familiar with it. As a Fire Chief the heroic commanding style of leadership works very well in a time of emergency. It centralizes command and final decision making. But before and after a 911 call, the shared leadership style in today's world is much more effective and far less exhausting. Being at the top is heavy burden to carry, why do it alone? While building a culture of trust is not exclusive to either style of leadership, it is easier to build and sustain when everyone feels responsible and empowered to hold that standard. To be effective as a leader you have to choose the type of leader you want to be. That style of leadership must be in alignment with your corporate core values and the type of capitalism you use to set goals and conduct your business transactions.

These are no small choices; these choices will shape you, your ability to lead and the fundamental nature of your company. Whether you build it to last (Collins 2001) or build it to sell it to someone else, it is part of your legacy and you can never get that time back. Think carefully; create a vision for yourself of the type of leader you want to be. Who are your heroes and why do you admire them? What type of companies inspires you—Clif Bar, Starbucks, WL Gore, Whole Foods, and Costco or more formal ones like IBM, Walgreens, Merck, and General Motors?

I want to go back to my example of Clif Bar for just one moment. Clif Bar has shared leadership with several outside CEOs and then back to that of owners Gary Erickson and his wife Kit Crawford as co-CEOs. The company itself is privately held with 80 percent owned by Gary and Kit and 20 percent by the employees in an ESOP. They are open and vulnerable to each other internally but not nearly as much with the outside business world. They do not share gross sales, net profits, or other financial details. Their culture or leadership thinking does not require them to do so. They make all the things (culture, leadership, and profitability) that would not seem possible using the old corporate capitalism work under social capitalism.

There are two important pieces to tie culture and leadership together and that's ownership and passion. In *Extreme Ownership* (Willink and Babin 2015), the authors put forth the premise that you are 100 percent responsible for your life and how you live it. Blaming others or circumstances for what happens to you only weakens you as a person and creates a victim mindset. My initial response when I read this was "sure, easy for Navy Seals to say," but on further reflection I decided this was one of those moments of surrender. I could take 100 percent ownership of my life or believe that others could dictate how my life should be. It's a choice and very empowering to take ownership. I've made the mistake of blaming others and didn't realize the impact it was having on me. I am unwilling to do that anymore, how about you?

Without passion for what you do, none of this work will amount to anything. People will see through you instead of wanting to follow you. Your passion for your business will connect you to all the other topics I have discussed so far, vulnerability, the head and heart connection, trust builders and trust killers, core values, the vulnerability scale, and the trust matrix. You will use all of these things in the step-by-step process to build trust between all your stakeholders.

Thoughts for Reflection

- Does the concept of social capitalism resonate with you?
- Are you more comfortable with traditional bottom-line, short-term results?
- Who do you want to attract to work in your business and why?
- What type of leader do you want to be?
- How important is it to your ego to be "in charge"?
- Has there ever been a time in your career where your status was more important than getting results?

CHAPTER 12

The Power of Conversation

Before you start a step-by-step process of building trust, two things need to happen first. After you read this book, everyone else you want involved in the process should read this book as well. This gives everyone involved in the conversation the common reference points, definitions, and contexts to discuss this effort. The second part is learning how to have very different types of conversations than what you are used to.

I believe society is losing the ability to have thoughtful, meaningful conversations on a daily basis. The divorce rate (at least in the United States) is well over 50 percent and one of the fundamental reasons cited for splitting up is a failure to communicate. In her book *Fierce Conversations*, Susan Scott says, "The conversation is the relationship." So basically when the conversation stops so does the relationship. If many of us are struggling to have good conversations in our personal lives, what makes you think your employees are going to be really good at conversation when they get to work?

I use personal relationship examples a lot in my work with my business clients because they have common reference points, ones that most people can relate to in one way or another. My wife and I are both in our second marriages as is probably at least half of your workforce. I've worked in conjunction with divorce mediators and marriage counselors when divorce threatens a business's future existence. I've seen marriage counselors often draw a diagram with two rings overlapping to show how a relationship is an entity and not just two people (Figure 12.1). The relationships in your business and with your employees and stakeholders are no different. The farther the two rings move apart, the overlap (entity/relationship) diminishes—until the relationship and emotional connection vanishes altogether.

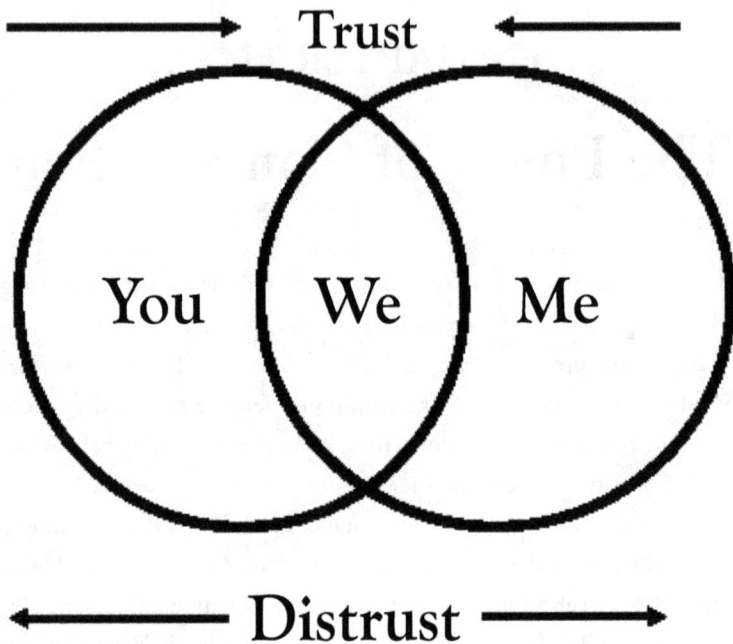

Figure 12.1 Trust circles

My wife Lisa and I both experienced how those circles were pulled apart in our prior marriages, until all trust was destroyed. Perhaps you have experienced this as well? The trust between two people (or lack thereof) is the fastest way to move these circles either closer together or to pull them apart. Without trust there can be no relationship, no meaningful conversation, and no connection. I've already covered what happens upon the betrayal of trust. Even seemingly simple white lies can build up over time to pull the circles apart. Each fracture of trust creates a greater pull in opposite directions, until it is nearly impossible to reverse the speed and direction. Some fractures are explosive; think back to Wells Fargo. The company had to make drastic changes to reverse the direction and spend millions of dollars rebuilding trust.

As the circles move farther apart, friction and frustration increase between employees. What often starts off as a simple misunderstanding can mushroom into full-blown anger, blame, and finger-pointing. Unresolved issues then become trigger points for future arguments, as the original root causes of the problem were never addressed. Lies are told and secrets are kept from each other. Employees feel they are not being listened to or respected. Betrayal of trust in the form of gossip is usually not far behind. So what can you do differently in your business to prevent this from happening? Learn how to talk and listen to each other in conversation, not just communication.

My wife and I both work and like to go out to dinner once a week to avoid cooking for at least one night. When we go out I look around the room and see couples sitting across from each other eating while staring off into space. At the next table is a family of four all looking at their phones instead of talking to each other. The average employee now spends at least five hours a day on the computer, reading and answering e-mails. Cell phones are mainly used for texting or using an app rather than an actual phone conversation. As one younger client recently said to me, "many of us avoid conversations because they are too intense and cause us a lot of stress or anxiety, texting is less stressful." Wait, what? Conversations are the catalyst for building the bonds of trust between individuals, then groups, then teams, divisions, and entire companies, and they are too stressful?

While working for TEC International in 2002, I had the opportunity to be in a workshop based on a book *The Communication Catalyst* (Connolly and Rianoshek 2002). The author's discussion of the power of conversation made me look at conversations very differently. Conversations can build upon each other in an upward, positive direction, "cycle of value," or take a negative downward destructive spiral, "cycle of waste." The conversations that take place while emotionally hijacked are a perfect example of the "cycle of waste. "They also had their own scale for measuring the quality of the conversation. At the low end of the scale was "Pretense" meaning the conversation was shallow and lacked substance. Pretense was a façade to hide behind so as not to be exposed or vulnerable to any degree to each other. At the top end of the scale was "Authenticity": conversations are just as the word implies, open to freely expressing yourself without fear of rejection or embarrassment. No pretense or protection is necessary.

If you look at the vulnerability scale you can see a close parallel of conversation to the degree of vulnerability. The quality of the conversation depends on the degree of vulnerability between those involved. Imagine just for a moment the positive impact to your business if everyone showed up to meetings authentically, feeling safe enough to share thoughts, ideas, and suggestions, free from the fear of judgment and embarrassment. What type of meetings do you believe you can have at that level of authenticity? I'll show you.

Communication and Conversation

I first want to make a distinction between communication and conversation in an organization. For this book I consider communication the transference of data and information, either between people or computers executing programs collecting or moving data. There is formal communication, what your organization says publicly, the content on your website, annual reports, company rules and procedures, your employee handbook, and any other communication which has the formal seal of approval. Then there is the informal communication that you don't want everyone to see or hear. Internal memos, sensitive information shared at meetings, or anything else you do not want put up on the company website.

Next are the formal and information conversations. While similar in intent they go deeper into creating the culture of trust. Formal conversations are those typically had in meetings, presentations, formal reviews, and so on. The informal conversations form the bulk of the actual conversations had on a daily basis. It used to be called "water cooler" talk, now it takes place around coffee machines, over cubicles, lunch break rooms, hallways, parking lots, online chat rooms, texts, and anywhere people meet personally or virtually outside of a "formal" environment. It is these conversations that generally form and bind the underlying corporate culture. It is here where senior employees share with newer ones "how things are really done around here." Gossip, innuendo, misinformation, back room power plays, politicking, bullying, and other conversation not meant for everyone takes place here, if you let it. My opinion based on thousands of hours of conversations and consulting with CEOs is that the bigger the gap between your formal conversations and informal conversations, the greater the distrust is inside the organization. I make a point of these as I have very strong feelings about the negative behavior which happens on a more informal basis or when those who should be exemplifying the standards for the formal rules look the other way. However, you have a wonderful opportunity to use informal networks for very positive things: employees' stories of their accomplishments outside of the workplace; saying thank you to those who have gone above and beyond to help co-workers or stakeholders; sharing thoughts, ideas, and suggestions of innovation, cost savings, quality improvement, or anything to improve the work quality of life. Remember, conversations are the relationship; use all the informal communication channels you have to keep everyone connected.

Different Levels of Conversations

Formal and informal conversations should abide by your core values. The real difference is in the structure and where they take place. All the conversations, however, should be had with the intention of respect deserved by everyone who works for you. In *Conversational Intelligence*, Judith Glaser breaks down conversations into three different categories: Level I (Tell–Ask), II (Inquire–Advocate), and Level III (Share–Discover). The level of trust required for each conversation ranges from low in Level I, conditional trust in Level II, and a high degree of trust in Level III. The differences in these conversations will be important in your future conversations in the step-by-step process of building trust in your organization. There is no right or wrong in these conversations. Each has its own place and degree of effectiveness in what you are trying to accomplish.

Level I conversations are important in many ways for keeping work on track and on time. More and more Level I conversations are completed via e-mail and texts rather than face to face. There is no question that face-to-face meetings can use up valuable time. However, e-mail is not appropriate in many instances where a phone conversation or face-to-face meeting is important for several reasons, nonverbal communication, and feeling connected.

The general belief over the years has been 55 percent of communication is body language, 38 percent is tone of voice, and 7 percent is the actual words spoken, and for me, emoticons are a poor representation of body language or facial expressions. Even if those numbers are slightly off, you have to be one heck of a writer to truly capture and convey all you want to say in an e-mail if it is anything more than transferring information. I don't know about you, but I have hundreds of examples of misconstrued e-mails that have caused unnecessary frustration, wasted time, anxiety, and hurt feelings. Perhaps you can think of a few of your own examples. Last thought on this, spelling, grammar, and punctuation do count and can completely change the context of the message. Be a stickler on this in your organization; it will pay great dividends. I've already talked about the connected feeling we get when talking face to face and to some extent over the phone. When face to face is not feasible for conversation due to time constraints or geography, I want you to think for a moment of the different feelings you would have communicating via e-mail, talking on the phone, or a video conference.

If you want to have a Level II conversation, try negotiating with a five-year-old! They are masters at inquiry (always asking why can't I?) and advocacy (persuading you to give them what they want). They are relentless in these conversations until they get a final no or you just get tired and give in! On an adult level however, this type of conversation rarely produces the results you want. Inquiring about another person's thoughts, ideas, or point of view is important, but not for the purpose of telling them why they are wrong and you are right. Listen to the news, politics, religion, gender, social welfare and reform, health care and many other topics that have become fertile ground for Level II conversations. Inquiry and advocacy are important conversational tools—until you get stuck there. Problems are outlined, fingers are pointed, blame is assigned—and nothing gets resolved.

Unfortunately, conversations often get stuck in Level II where a high value is placed on conditional trust (you have to earn my trust). This tends to happen in meetings a lot where no one feels safe enough to show up authentically and ask the tough questions for fear of being shown wrong or worse, getting wacked. Have you ever been in a conversation with someone when as soon as it started you knew exactly where it would end? I'm right, you're wrong, and I will prove to you just how wrong you really are! These types of conversations are counterproductive, forcing the participants to defend their positions rather than finding solutions to the challenges being faced. Here, trust is often destroyed by careless or hurtful comments and actions. The circles in the relationship diagram often get pulled further and further apart by Level II conversations.

Level III conversations by their very nature are designed to be different. These conversations are where the real emotionally mature adults show up to inquire, share, discover, and create incredible value. I personally get excited just thinking about them and look forward to every opportunity to engage in these conversations with others. There is safe space, little or no judgment, no pretense and the vulnerability that opens the door to cocreating.

It is these conversations that create the connectedness most human beings crave. Scientific research clearly defines the effect our mirror neurons have on our emotions. You can literally feel someone else's fear, joy, sorry, pain, frustration, anger, or anxiety. At the start, these conversations happen much more by design than they do by default, until they become habit in your organization. Level III conversations will play a critical role in the steps to building trust and impact all the future conversations within your company. Envision the shift that could take place by moving conversations from telling and debating to creating. What could you accomplish?

Thoughts for Reflection

- How productive would your staff rate your meetings?
- Have you ever avoided important conversations by sending a text or e-mail instead?
- How much time do you spend advocating your points of view?
- Who in the room needs to be right?
- Who doesn't share much out of fear of getting wacked?
- How often do you leave meetings with actionable solutions?
- On a scale of 1 to 100, what's the level of trust between the people in the room?
- Do you believe the level of trust stays constant or changes depending on the topic of discussion?

CHAPTER 13

Thoughts, Words, and Deeds

I know I have covered a lot of material in this book. I've discussed how being vulnerable is not a weakness but takes courage and personal strength to expose yourself to others to any degree; how giving and receiving trust is different and why; the actions that can create trust and how easily it can be broken, even with a simple white lie; the importance of forgiveness and letting go of the emotional connection to past hurts that hold you back; identifying and defining your core values; the incredible connection between your heart and your head and the alignment between the two; and creating tools called the vulnerability scale and the trust matrix and how to use them in your business.

All of the chapters have been designed to build on each other and lead you to the point where you have all the understanding and foundational building blocks you need to create trust in your culture. I hope you have been keeping a journal while reading this book and taken the time to answer the questions for reflection at the end of each chapter. Those notes will be very useful as I lay out the steps I believe necessary to create and sustain trust in your business.

The Gap

There can be a real gap between reading, understanding, and then actually doing what you've read about. Actually doing many of the things I've outlined in this book may feel awkward or clumsy and when it comes to forgiveness just impossible to do. So the first thing I am going to tell you to do is breathe and relax. Uncomfortable feelings tend to cause most people to procrastinate; who wants to start something that creates negative feelings? The second big reason most people don't start a new initiative is the fear of being embarrassed. What if this doesn't work, what if I fall flat on my face? I can assure you there will be missteps along the way. So what? Give yourself permission now to step out and take risks, fail at times, learn, adapt, and move on. Not taking yourself too seriously is an excellent place to start; it makes others feel safe when you are not perfect. Humility will create more admiration and respect from others than contempt.

Start now. I have worked with many people who procrastinate by waiting for the sun, moon, and stars to all line up, or for the perfect "tool" to come along. In *Think and Grow Rich*, Napoleon Hill says, "Start where you stand, and work with whatever tools you have at your command, better tools will be found as you go." Your heart, your mind, and your voice are the perfect instruments to begin the process.

The Steps

Now you will need a note book and the steps outlined below. You don't have to write a novel or a 50-page business plan; keep it simple and most importantly capture your feelings about the process along the way. It will help keep you connected to the work and allow others to feel connected when the Level III conversations start.

Step 1:
- Determine all of the people you want to start the discussion about creating a culture of trust.
- Have every one of them read this book and create their own person journal (this is a must).
- Make a personal commitment to see this process through.
- Designate one person involved in this process to be your Chief Trust Officer. They will have the authority to stop the process if they feel you are getting off track.
- Set up a timeline for everyone to read this book and then a specific meeting date to discuss:
    - What parts of the book resonated for them the most?
    - What were their individual core values?
    - What resentments and other barriers to building trust are they still hanging on to?
    - What do they feel will be the real benefits to the organization by building a culture of trust?

Step 2:

- Make sure everyone is on track for finishing the book with their notes prior to the meeting.
- Set up a meeting space where you are free from distractions, phones, interruptions, or day-to-day operations.
- I suggest you allot at least four hours for your initial meeting. There is a meeting outline included to give you an idea on how to make the best use of your time.
- Bring in breakfast or lunch depending on the time of day. I have found conversations never go well on an empty stomach. Nothing heavy or overly caffeinated, either you will get drowsy or hyperactive. I had one CEO get so nervous about the discussion he didn't sleep well the night before, drank a lot of coffee to get going, and the dozed off two-thirds of the way through the meeting.

Step 3:

- Your first meeting is very important and sets the ground work for everything you do going forward.
- Use the outline I created or develop one of your own, but have a clear plan in place for what you are going to do.
- You and your collective group's ability to have collaborative, creative conversations (Level III) will determine the rate of speed at which changes occur.
- I keep President Harry S. Truman's quote posted: "It is amazing what you can accomplish if you do not care who gets the credit." Being emotional and passionate about a topic is great until the ego kicks in. Egos must get checked at the door to the room as much as possible. Remember, you all win or lose as a team.
- If the meeting gets too hot, take a break, breathe, relax, and come back to it. These types of conversations take practice to stay focused and productive. Once you learn to do them well, you will not want to go back to the old style of meetings.

1. Face-to-face meetings are the most effective for starting the trust conversations. Participants can feel what is going on for each other;

video conferencing causes too much isolation and allows for distractions during the meeting.

2. Find a meeting/conference room large enough to hold the 20-person team with freedom to move around the room. If you have a room like this that's great if there are no distractions, if not then find an offsite location.

3. Breakfast should be available at 7.30 a.m. and the meeting will start at 8 a.m. sharp. Sharing a meal tends to put people at ease prior to starting a meeting. You can do lunch for afternoon half-day session. One of the most enjoyable workshops I've done started with lunch, went to 5.30 p.m., and then ended with dinner to debrief and decompress. It made for a late night and a very productive day. You get to choose for your team.

4. Regardless of start time, all members of the team are notified to be on time (that means arrive ½ hour prior to start).

5. The workshop template (Table 13.1) starts with breakfast and will end at 12.30 p.m. Lunch will be available at the end. The idea is to encourage them to stay and continue their conversations (at a new level) rather than running back to their desks.

6. You will need several flip charts, at least one for each five people, markers for each, and necessary number of tables and chairs. Your team should be broken up into tables of four or five team members each and they choose a spokesperson for the first segment.

7. You can do the facilitation yourself or bring in a professional like me. Caveat: doing it yourself will make it very difficult to fully participate and facilitate at the same time.

Table 13.1 Half-day workshop setup

Agenda:	
Time	**Agenda item—facilitators' guide**
8–8.05 a.m.	CEO welcome to the team (CEO is prepared to cover why the team is doing this workshop now that everyone has read the book)
8.05–8.25 a.m.	Team members introduce themselves, what they do for the company, how long with company, one thing they would like to learn today

8.25–8.35 a.m.	Create Rules of Engagement (ROE) for this workshop (have examples of "Rules" from the book and get these written down and posted on the wall. Part 2 of the conversation is "what are the consequences if a rule is broken?" Biggest offender is being late after breaks. Be creative with the consequence, not punitive, that is, a person has to tell a joke, sing a song, anything that pushes them out of their comfort zone in a fun way
8.35–8.40 a.m.	A quick review of Conversational Intelligence three levels of conversations (Levels I, II, III) and an agreement to stay at Level III. Make it one of the rules of engagement and all participants agree that a time out will be called by anyone who feels the group is stuck at a Level I or Level II conversation
8.40–8.50 a.m.	Icebreaker: Open discussion—what parts of the book resonated the most for you and why? Capture salient points on a flip chart
8.50–9.20 a.m.	Core values discussion—setting the compass with core values as the guiding principles for the organization. Team members can share their individual core values and CEO shares core values for the organization. How many align and where are their possible conflicts?
9.20–9.50 a. m.	The corporate core values are posted together with definition as it applies to how everything we do going forward will be measured against those values. If there is a conflict either we change what we are doing to be aligned with the value or we stop doing it
9.50–10.15 a.m.	Time for a break—you will need it before the next conversations over the trust matrix for each member. One team member should be responsible for watching the time and starting on time—remember the Rules of Engagement
10.15–10.45 a.m.	Trust matrix conversations—this can be a tough part of the workshop. Each team member should have received copies of their assessments by the other team members ahead of time, to read, get over any shocks, digest, and reflect. This starts as a table-top discussion to make it more intimate rather than in front of the entire room. Cover the following points: Initial emotional reactions What did you agree with? What did you disagree with? What resentments are you holding onto? How did your feelings about each team member change? Anything else you want to say?
10.45–11.00 a.m.	Rapid recall—go around the room quickly and each team member has the opportunity to express how they felt at the beginning of the table discussion and at the end. One thing they learned about themselves. This gives everyone an opportunity to talk and decompress a little bit
11.00–11.15 a.m.	Moving onto creating something real positive—Aspirations conversation—each table has a conversation around where do you want to be on the vulnerability scale with your team members. Write down where you think you are now and what it will take to move the needle up on the scale. Capture important points on the flip chart

(Continued)

Table 13.1 Half-day workshop setup (Continued)

Agenda:	
Time	**Agenda item—facilitators' guide**
11.15–11.30 a.m.	Each table spokesperson summarizes their table's conversation, where they are now, and how the needle can be moved. After each summary the flip chart should be posted on the wall
11.30–11.50 a.m.	Commitments to action: What is the one critical thing each team member will do in the next 30 days to build on what we accomplished today? What is the one thing each team member will do differently going forward to advance the needle on their vulnerability scale? Each team member can be paired up with an accountability partner. The partners and the commitments will be recorded and signed off on the flip chart
11.50–12.00 p.m.	CEO commitment to seeing this process through. Scheduling next meetings weekly, monthly, quarterly, and so on. Designate team members to take on different tasks for this process, scheduling, consolidating the flip charts into notes, creating agenda, creating graphics around the corporate core values. Create a "Move the Needle" campaign and measure the results. Keep it fun and creative!
12.00–12.30 p.m.	CEO thank you and lunch conversations

This is just a template, and a very aggressive one for the time allotted. Almost any format can be used except winging it.

Step 4:

With the first meeting finished you now should have an outline and timeline for your organization. Weekly, Monthly, and Quarterly meetings should be set for staying on track and making the necessary adjustments required for your plan to stay viable. Creating trust requires time, patience, understanding, and commitment. You have to deconstruct what already exists and rebuild it the way that you want it to be.

The Virtual Workforce

Physically getting all your people together for these meetings may not be possible. I had no idea when I started writing this book how true that statement would become. I feel I would be remiss if I didn't address the challenges the world faces right now during the COVID-19 pandemic. I live and work on Long Island, NY, right between two hospitals overwhelmed with virus patients and thousands are dying on a daily basis. All of us in this area are now in our fourth week of "sheltering in place," working from home when possible, practicing "social distancing" in an effort to "flatten the curve," all new terms not used until now. Millions have been laid off from work and companies are scrambling to set up employees to work virtually. You can't assume your employees have a computer and Internet at home to work this way. The question becomes, how do I keep my staff connected, keep the morale up, and all of us working together when none of us can be in the same building? I reached out to the CEOs I know and asked what they are doing during this unprecedented time. Here are some of the great things they are doing now to help keep it all together:

- Video huddles: Staff meet virtually at least three times a week either in the morning or lunchtime via video conference. The calls last 30 minutes to 1 hour depending on what is going on. We share how everyone is feeling, personal stories, concerns, who needs anything, and go over the punch list of things done and to do for the next call.
- Some companies use an evergreen Google Hangout Chat called "The Water Cooler" where anyone at any time can hop on and chat with peers while working. They talk to other people in the company they would not normally talk to.
- Other chat rooms included Microsoft Teams, Slack, and Salesforce chatter.
- Virtual Happy Hours was a very common response, people grab their favorite beverage and get on the call. You can leave the call anytime you want.

Other ideas:

- Virtual dinner parties
- Lunch and Learn programs via webinar
- Guided meditation
- Exercising at home instead of the gym
- Proper nutrition for mental health

The overarching theme was to over-communicate and create a bit of transparency that would otherwise not exist because everyone is separated. As one CEO shared:

> Be informative, empathetic, and clear when you are sharing opinions versus providing data. In general, just show that you care about everyone and make them feel like stakeholders in everything that you are going through together as a company. You also have to keep in mind that everyone is cooped up all day, so we as (CEOs) have a responsibility to try to keep everyone positive and as happy as they can be. Mental health is crucial right now both for sanity and to stay healthy and avoid the worst aspects of the virus that stress can trigger. (Weinstein 2020)

Leading Change

A word of caution, don't do it alone. Many leaders, especially in the heroic style, have the urge to step in and push the process faster if you're not getting the results you want. It is imperative that all employees at some point be engaged in the process. Unexpected barriers and resistance will come up, of that you can be certain. It will take a creative collaboration to find solutions.

Why is this so important? Distrust and control often go hand in hand. Your desire to control people, places, and things to create the outcomes you want may become so strong that you give off the signal, "I don't trust anyone to (fill in the blank) as well as I can." Remember the chapter on confusing competence, confidence, and trust? Control is a prime example of how confusing your feelings or judgments around competence or confidence can cause severe misunderstandings. Competence is about skill sets and abilities; trust is a surrender of control. A wise guru I was introduced to put it succinctly, "There is no negotiation in surrender."

The deepest levels of trust—90 or higher on the trust scale—often require your full surrender in trusting your direct reports, employees, and other stakeholders. If they are truly worthy of your trust, are you willing to give it? This lies at the heart of creating a trusting culture. Your organization consists of a continuous flow of relationships between all of your employees. There is a pulse, an energy created when groups of people come together. Your culture is born out of that energy or the force that binds all of us together.

The Ties That Bind

It takes two or more people to create a relationship and form the ties that bind us, that sense of connectedness. All stakeholders are responsible for keeping the relationship alive and well; this requires ownership. Two halves do not make a whole; you will note two full circles in the diagram that merge to form a third entity. I don't believe any group or team of people will form a perfect overlap. We are all human; we make mistakes and say or do dumb things at times. Those circles will be in constant flux; the goal is to have them not move too far apart and trust is the force that pulls them closer together.

Thoughts for Reflection

- When was the last time you had a large gap between knowing what to do and being able to do it?
- What steps did you take to close the gap? What worked? What did not go as planned?
- What was the last change initiative you started but did not finish? What was the biggest challenge?
- What are your plans for working a virtual or partially virtual workforce?
- If money were no object what changes would you make right now in your business?

Epilogue

This book is not meant to be the final word on trust, in fact just the opposite. I want this book to be the catalyst for starting what I hope are many future conversations between people and more writing on this subject. I believe the discussion of trust is that important.

I am not the same man I was when I started my journey to write this book. It has been a labor of love, passion, and an incredible sorting process of my own thoughts, ideas, and intuition. The conversations I have had with others while writing and researching have brought me closer to people than I ever thought possible.

I have made the argument that trust is the most important value you can create in your organization. It gives you a competitive edge by attracting the type of people you want working in your business and lets them feel good about the company they work for; profitability follows.

Whether you choose to have a corporate or social capitalistic model, be a heroic or shared leader, the most important thing is making conscious decisions. Be clear about what you want and why. Do not follow what others are doing just because they tell you how successful they have been. They are not you—different person, different company, and usually different economic times.

Tough choices do become a little easier with clarity and focus. There is no perfect science to creating or changing any process involving people. You and those who work for you will make mistakes. Reframe the mistake, forgive, learn from it, and make a better decision.

Don't do it alone. Build a circle of people you can trust to work through the toughest of challenges; not everyone in your organization may be up for this change in culture. Seek out wise counsel from those who have already begun this process; ask for help when you need it. Remember being vulnerable requires strength and courage. It is not a sign of weakness.

Trust between people is what gives each of you the ability to have meaningful relationships, build amazing businesses, be more effective

CEOs, and enjoy the work you do even more for the benefit of all stake-holders. Trust will allow all those involved in this process to connect to your vision and passion—to reach your goals. As a CEO or business owner, I hope you will join me in building a community of like-minded individuals who are open to being vulnerable enough to share the challenges you face real time in creating trust in your organization. To that end I would like to hear from you including:

- Your thoughts on trust in the workplace or trust in general.
- What has worked for you in building trust and what has not?
- Suggestions for adding to the Thoughts for Reflection.
- Any other comments you want to share.

Call or e-mail me if you need help getting started with the steps for building trust in your business. My contact information is in the back of this book. It's never too late to start these conversations with your staff. Take ownership of the opportunity this book offers, choose a path, and together, let's make it happen, starting right now.

References

Introduction

Brown, B. 2018. *Dare to Lead*. New York, NY: Penguin Random House LLC.

Claveria, K. 2019. "On the Brink of Distrust: A New Study Urges Companies to Engage Customers and Employees." *Vision Critical* https://visioncritical.com/blog/2017-trust-barometer

Covey, S.M., ed. 2008. *The Speed of Trust*. New York, NY: Free Press, Division of Simon and Shuster.

Sisodia, R., J. Sheth, and D. Wolfe. 2014. *Firms of Endearment*. New Jersey, NJ: Pearson Education.

Chapter 1

Chamine, S. 2016. *Positive Intelligence*. Austin: Greenleaf Book Group Press.

Edmondson, A.C. 2019. *The Fearless Organization, Creating Psychological Safety in the Workplace for Learning, Innovation, and Growth*. Hoboken: John Wiley & Sons, Inc.

Shechtman, M.R. 1998. *The Internal Frontier: Creating the Personal Transformations That Lead to Success*. Los Angeles: New Star Press.

Sifferlin, A. 2017. "13% of Americans Take Antidepressants." *Time* https://time.com/4900248/antidepressants-depression-more-common

The Arbinger Institute. 2010. *Leadership and Self-Deception, Getting Out of the Box*. San Francisco: BerrettKoehler.

Vennie, Q. 2017. "Entrepreneur." https://entrepreneur.com/article/290530

Willink, J., and L. Babin. 2015. *Extreme Ownership, How U.S. Navy Seals Lead and Win*. New York, NY: St. Martin's Press.

Chapter 2

Bulwer-Lytton, E. 1839. *Richelieu; or The Conspiracy: A Play in Five Acts*. London: Saunders and Otley.

Glaser, J.E. 2014. *Conversational Intelligence, How Great Leaders Build Trust and Get Extraordinary Results* Brookline: Bibliomotion, Inc.

Grodnitzky, G.R. 2014. *Culture Trumps Everything*. MountainFrog Publishing.

Hill, N. 1996. *Think and Grow Rich*. New York: Ballantine Books, Division of Random House, Inc.

Logan, D. J. King, and H. Fisher-Wright. 2008. *Tribal Leadership, Leveraging Natural Groups to Build a Thriving Organization*. New York, NY: HarperCollins.

Scott, S. 2002 *Fierce Conversations*, New York, NY: Viking Penguin.

Chapter 3

Brown, B. 2018. *Dare to Lead*. New York, NY: Penguin Random House LLC.

Covey, S.M.R. ed. 2008 *The Speed of Trust*. New York, NY: Free Press, Division of Simon and Shuster.

Kahneman, D. 2011. *Thinking, Fast and Slow*. New York, NY: Farrar, Straus and Giroux.

Staley, O. 2016. "Culture Clash, Wells Fargo Just Became the Poster Child for When External and Internal Values Don't Match." *Quartz*, September 1, https://qz.com/777241/wells-fargos-fake-accounts-scandal-makes-it-the-perfect-poster-child-for-when-external-and-internal-values-dont-match

Chapter 4

Alcohol Anonymous World Services, Inc. 2002 *Twelve Steps and Twelve Traditions*.

Chopra, D., D. Ford, and M. Williamson. 2010. *The Shadow Effect: Illuminating the Hidden Power of Your True Self*. New York, NY: HarperCollins.

Goleman, D., R. Boyatzis and A. McKee. 2002. *Primal Leadership Realizing the Power of Emotional Intelligence*. Boston: Harvard Business School Press.

Lusking, F. 2002. *Forgive for Good: A Proven Prescription for Health and Happiness*. New York, NY: HarperCollins.

Ramis, H.D. 1993. *Groundhog Day*. Woodstock, Ill: Columbia Pictures.

Turner, D.E. Seattle Times Columnist and Congregational Minister.

Chapter 5

Baden-Powell, R. 2004. *Scouting for Boys The Original 1908 Edition*. Oxford: Oxford University Press.

George, B. 2007. *True North: Discover your Authentic Leadership*. San Francisco: Josey-Bass A Wiley Imprint.

Kahneman, D. 2011. *Thinking, Fast and Slow*. New York, NY: Farrar, Straus and Giroux.

McCraty, R., M. Atkinson, D. Tomasino, R. Bradley. 2009. *The Coherent Heart, Heart-Brain Interactions, Psychophysiological Coherence, and the Emergence of System-Wide Order*. Integral Review.

Chapter 6

Caulkin, S. 2008. "Gore-Tex gets made Without Managers." *The Guardian*, https://theguardian.com/business/2008/nov/02/gore-tex-textiles-terri-kelly

Collins, J. 2001. *Good to Great* New York, NY: HarperCollins.

Porter, M.E. 1998. *Competitive Advantage, Creating and Sustain Superior Performance*. New York, NY: FreePress, Division of Simon and Schuster.

Chapter 7

Augsburger, D.W. 1982. *Caring Enough to Hear and Be Heard*. Ventura, Baker Publishing Group.

Berne, E.M.D. 1973. *Games People Play*. New York, NY: Ballantine Books, a Division of Random House, Inc.

Brown, B. 2018. *Dare to Lead*. New York, NY: Penguin Random House LLC.

Crowley, R., and V. Kublis. 2012. *Imagine All Better: How to Easily Break Repeating Behavior Patterns*. San Francisco: Cahill House Publishing.

Drake, D.B. 2018. *Narrative Coaching: The Definitive Guide to Bringing New Stories to Life*. Petaluma: CNC Press.

Frankel, V. 1984. *Man's Search for Meaning*. Boston: Beacon Press.

Franklin, B. 2016. *The Complete Illustrated History The Autobiography of Benjamin Franklin*. Minneapolis: Voyageur Press, an imprint of Quarto Publishing Group.

Glaser, J.E. 2014. *Conversational Intelligence, How Great Leaders Build Trust and Get Extraordinary Results*. Brookline: Bibliomotion, Inc.

Goleman, D., R. Boyatzis, and A. McKee. 2002. *Primal Leadership Realizing the Power of Emotional Intelligence*. Boston: Harvard Business School Press.

Grodnitzky, G.R. 2014. *Culture Trumps Everything*. MountainFrog Publishing.

Kahneman, D. 2011. *Thinking, Fast and Slow*. New York, NY: Farrar, Straus and Giroux.

Kwik, J. 2019. *How to Develop a Super Memory*. Mindvalley Master Class.

Lencioni, P. 1998. *The Five Temptations of a CEO*. San Francisco: Josey-Bass A Wiley Imprint.

Mountain, D.O. 2001. *The Invitation* San Francisco: HarperOne.

Ruiz, D.M. 1997. *The Four Agreements*. San Rafael: Amber-Allen Publishing, Inc.

Senge, P. 1990. *The Fifth Discipline: The Art and Practice of the Learning Organization*. New York, NY: Doubleday, a division of Bantam Doubleday Dell Publishing Group, Inc.

Chapter 8

None

Chapter 9

Branden, N. 1998. *Self-Esteem at Work, How Confident People Make Powerful Companies.* San Francisco: Josey-Bass.

Chapter 10

Clif Bar 2020. https://clifbar.com/who-we-are/our-aspirations

Lagaorio, C. 2018. Inc. https://inc.com/christine-lagorio-chafkin/2018-private-titans-clif-bar-investors-money.html

Chapter 11

Goleman, D., R. Boyatzis and A. McKee. 2002. *Primal Leadership Realizing the Power of Emotional Intelligence.* Boston: Harvard Business School Press.

Grodnitzky, G.R. 2014. *Culture Trumps Everything.* MountainFrog Publishing

Willink, J., and L. Babin. 2015. *Extreme Ownership, How U.S. Navy Seals Lead and Win.* New York, NY: St. Martin's Press.

Chapter 12

Connolly, M., and R. Rianoshek. 2002. *The Communication Catalyst,* Illinois: Dearborn Trade Publishing, a Kaplan Professional Company.

Glaser, J.E. 2014. *Conversational Intelligence, How Great Leaders Build Trust and Get Extraordinary Results* Brookline: Bibliomotion, Inc.

Scott, S. 2002. *Fierce Conversations,* New York, NY: Viking Penguin.

Chapter 13

Hill, N. 1996. *Think and Grow Rich.* New York, NY: Ballantine Books, Division of Random House, Inc.

Logan, D., J. King and H. Fisher-Wright. 2008. *Tribal Leadership, Leveraging Natural Groups to Build a Thriving Organization.* New York, NY: HarperCollins.

Weinstein, E.R. 2020. *Virtual Workforce Connectedness- Ideas for Keeping Employees Connected During a Pandemic.* This comment is from my discussion notes of a CEO group meeting in April 2020. It is not published anywhere. Not sure how to reference this.

About the Author

Russell J. von Frank II, MBA, EMT, CEO, author, executive coach, trainer, speaker, and business consultant. Starting off as a Third Officer in the U.S. Merchant Marine and Ensign in the U.S. Navy Reserve he went on to be third generation CEO of his family business. After 25 years he merged that business with another to spend more time on executive coaching and business consulting. Over 20 years he has logged in over 10,000 hours of coaching and consulting business leaders of all size companies and industries. He holds two Bachelor of Science degrees, an MBA in Organizational Development, and coaching certifications in Conversational Intelligence, Positive Intelligence and Global Team Coaching.

In his free time Russ is a volunteer firefighter and EMT. He is an Ex-Chief of his community fire department. He is also a three time past president of two different Rotary Clubs.

Russ can be reached via email at russ@russvonfrank.com or through his website www.russvonfrank.com. He would love to hear your thoughts, ideas and stories on this subject.

Index

OTHER TITLES IN THE BUSINESS CAREER DEVELOPMENT COLLECTION

Vilma Barr, Consultant, Editor

- *Innovative Selling* by Eden White
- *Present! Connect!* by Tom Guggino
- *Introduction to Business* by Patrice Flynn
- *Be Different!* by Stan Silverman

Announcing the Business Expert Press Digital Library

Concise e-books business students need for classroom and research

This book can also be purchased in an e-book collection by your library as

- a one-time purchase,
- that is owned forever,
- allows for simultaneous readers,
- has no restrictions on printing, and
- can be downloaded as PDFs from within the library community.

Our digital library collections are a great solution to beat the rising cost of textbooks. E-books can be loaded into their course management systems or onto students' e-book readers.
The **Business Expert Press** digital libraries are very affordable, with no obligation to buy in future years. For more information, please visit **www.businessexpertpress.com/librarians**. To set up a trial in the United States, please email **sales@businessexpertpress.com.**